WHITE SUPREMACY IN JAPAN: A MEMOIR

———————

WHITE SUPREMACY IN JAPAN: A MEMOIR

Pierce Parker

CreateSpace
an Amazon company

This publication is designed to provide accurate and
authoritative information in regard to the subject
matter covered. It is sold with the understanding that
the publisher is not engaged in rendering legal, accounting,
or other professional service. If legal advice or other
expert assistance is required, the services of a
competent professional person should be sought.
From a Declaration of Principles jointly adopted by a
Committee of the American Bar Association and a Committee of Publishers.

Library of Congress Cataloging in Publication Data

Parker, Pierce C. (Pierce Christopher)
    White Supremacy in Japan: A Memoir

        Bibliography: p.
        Includes index.
        1. Modern Japanese Society.   I. Title.

        ISBN-13: 978-1500435691
        ISBN-10: 1500435694

        Printed in the United States of America

10 9 8 7 6 5 4 3 2 1

I dedicate this book to Christina E. Guilbert who had no way of knowing the events described herein, and as a consequence, has lost me forever.

What is sometimes called the national "psyche" was formed by a variety of factors and circumstances through the centuries. An exploration of the nature of those factors, make it possible to gain some insight into the "spirit" of a nation.

- Oleksander Kulchytsky

Unethical and illegal actions do not go undetected forever.

From *Management Mistakes and Successes,* by Robert F. Hartley, p. 225

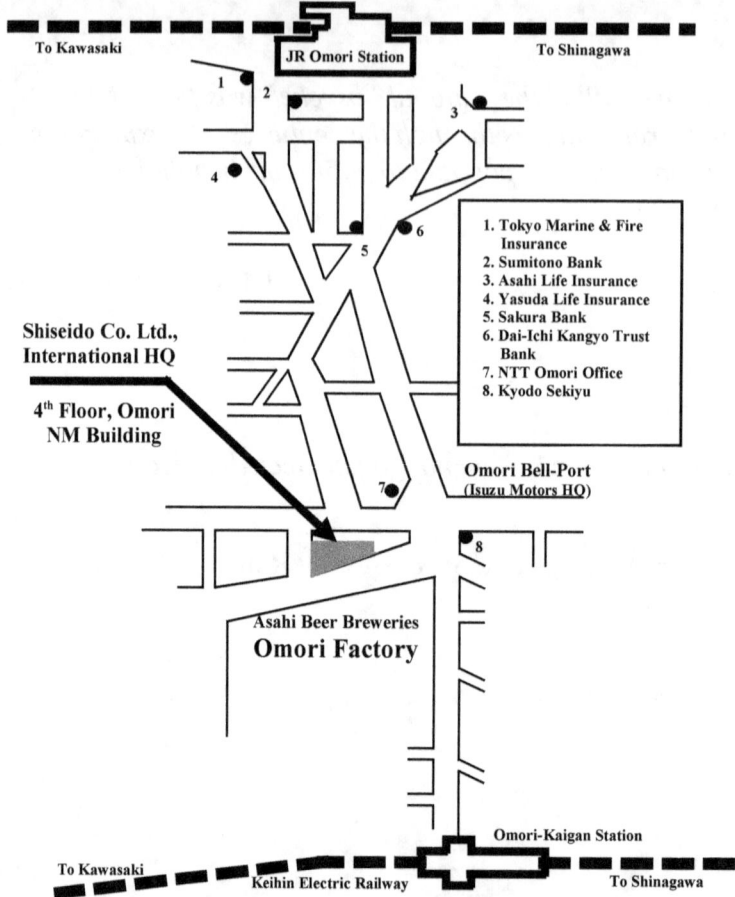

To Kawasaki

JR Omori Station

To Shinagawa

1
2
3
4
5
6

1. Tokyo Marine & Fire
   Insurance
2. Sumitono Bank
3. Asahi Life Insurance
4. Yasuda Life Insurance
5. Sakura Bank
6. Dai-Ichi Kangyo Trust
   Bank
7. NTT Omori Office
8. Kyodo Sekiyu

**Shiseido Co. Ltd.,
International HQ**

**4th Floor, Omori
NM Building**

Omori Bell-Port
(Isuzu Motors HQ)

7
8

**Asahi Beer Breweries
Omori Factory**

Omori-Kaigan Station

To Kawasaki

Keihin Electric Railway

To Shinagawa

The Guide to Shiseido Omori International Headquarters

Contents

Table of Names...10
Introduction...13
White Supremacy in Japanese Society...17
July 12, 1998...23
Hidden Penalties...26
Oscar Godoy..31
White Women in Japan...42
The Managers...65
Employment Contract Renewal Negotiation...72
Epilog..80
Appendices..86
   TO: Monica Lennie..92
   Employment contract..93
   "American Gigolo" 97
   Fond Memories of Life with a Host Family.....................................99
   SECTIONS: The Land of the Rising Crom....................................102
   Ethnic Japanese find tightly closed society...................................104
Index...107
Bibliography..108

White Supremacy in Japan:
A Memoir

_____

With Our Employees

The individuals who make up our work force - in all their diversity and creativity - are our most valuable corporate asset. We strive to promote their professional development and to evaluate them fairly. We recognize the importance of their personal satisfaction and well-being, and seek to grow together with them.

With Our Society

We respect and obey all laws in all regions in which we do business. Safety and preservation of the natural environment are our highest priorities. In cooperation with local communities and in harmony with international society, we call on our cultural resources in creating a global, beautiful, cultured lifestyle.

The Shiseido Way was enacted in 1997 and better clarifies what is expected of each Shiseido employee in his/her daily activities in regard to our customers, our business partners, our shareholders, and society as a whole.

Reprinted from http://www.shiseido.co.jp/e/e9711way/html/way00002.htm

Table of Names

This book is based on a true story. Names of some characters may have been changed to protect their privacy. Titles have been added to non-Indo-European names to clarify the gender.

In the International Business Department II, Omori International Headquarters
Mr. Toru ARAI
· Director of the European and New Markets Section in the International Business Department II.

Mr. ASADA
· Employee in the International Business Department II.

Jean-Christian DE LA CHEVALERIE
· French expatriate, stationed in the International Business Department II.
· Was responsible for opening new markets in Saudi Arabia and Lebanon.

Olivier JAPIOT
· French intern from *L'École Nationale d'Administration* between September, 1993 and January, 1994

Mr. MIYAZAKI
· In charge of the Irish market in the International Business Department II.

Mr. Yoshiyuki NAGAI
· General Manager of the International Business Department II.

Anne NEUMANN
· American expatriate, stationed in the International Department II.
· Was responsible for the markets in Portugal, Denmark, and Sweden.

Ms. SHIOYA
· In charge of CARITA, SA, a Shiseido subsidiary in France.

Mr. SUGITA
· Employee in the International Business Department II.

Mr. Masaharu TAKAHASHI
· Deputy General Manager of the International Business Department II.

In the Marketing Department, Omori International HQ
Yael ALKALAY
· American expatriate, stationed in the advertising/creative section of the Marketing Department.

Carolyn LATTIN
· American expatriate, stationed in the Marketing Department.

Shiseido Nippacho Research Laboratory Center in Nippacho, Kanagawa Prefecture
Oscar GODOY
· "English" teacher at the Shiseido Nippacho Research Laboratory Center.
· Personal friend of Dr. Tatsuya Ozawa.

Dr. Tatsuya OZAWA
· Senior Executive Director of the Shiseido Nippacho Research Laboratory Center.

Shiseido Nippacho Mes Amis Dormitory in Nippacho, Kanagawa Prefecture
Mr. Yukihara KANDA
· Residential Director at Shiseido Nippacho *Mes Amis* dormitory.

Dr. Takahiko SUWA
· Ph.D. resident at Shiseido Nippacho *Mes Amis* dormitory.

Mr. Ryo YAMANISHI
· My next door neighbor at Shiseido Nippacho *Mes Amis* dormitory.
· Worked in the Information System Department.

In the Human Resources Department, Ginza Main Building
Mr. Shuzo SHIMOJO
· General Manager at Human Resources Department.

Mr. SAKUMA
· Director at Human Resources Department.

Ms. Miki ISHIWATA
· Deputy Director at Human Resources Department.

Dana JOURDAN
· German expatriate, stationed in the Human Resources Department.

In the Legal Department, Ginza Main Building
Cameron BROWN
· American expatriate, stationed in the Patent/Legal Department.
· One of the original "Shiseido Girls."

Ms. Yoko DOI
· Employee in the Legal Department.

Mr. Shiro EMORI
· Deputy General Manager of the Legal Department

Ms. Mimi GUMELATY
· Indonesian expatriate, stationed in the Legal Department.

Mr. Ryozo MORI
· General Manager of the Legal Department.

Diane HASE
· American expatriate, stationed in the Legal Department.

Mr. Akira SEKI
· Employee in the Legal Department.

In the Public Relations Department, Ginza Main Building
Mr. SUGIYAMA
· General Manager of the Public Relations Department.

CHAPTER 1

Introduction

We are creatures of the past and memory, and we chart our future based on the events of the past. One of the major characteristics that distinguishes humans from other species is that people have a significantly greater capacity to learn, remember and think about what has happened in the past, is happening in the present, and might happen in the future.[1] I often think about the time and the experience I had in Japan. I was employed by a giant cosmetics firm, Shiseido Cosmetics, and I have lived and worked in Japan from July of 1993 to November of 1994. I was in Japan once again during the last week of June in 1996 on a business trip, and I was absolutely engulfed by the nostalgic memories of that country. I would suppose we would prefer to go back to the places where we have had fond memories of; thus, when I was in Japan once again, I realized how much I abhorred that country and what bad memories I had of that Asian nation. There were that ubiquitous smell of burning fish, filthy streets, and most of all, the unbearably hot humid weather. Looking back, I could not readily express what exactly was going through my mind when I abruptly resigned from Shiseido and left Japan in November of 1994. This book is to offer some explanations on my psychological state and motives at the time. When I abruptly left Japan in November of 1994, I was absolutely sick of the country, and I never wanted to go back there ever again. In many ways, going to Japan to live and work was my personal Vietnam in a sense that I did so purely out of gaining "prestige." First, I did not have a clear purpose as to why I was going to Japan. Was I going to Japan to live and work permanently? Or was I to stay in Japan only for a short while, save as much money as possible and return to the U. S.? I still can not answer these two questions now, and I certainly have

---

[1] - Cook, Curtis W., Hunsaker, Phillip L. and Coffey, Robert E. *Management and Organizational Behavior,* 2nd Edition, IRWIN/McGraw-Hill. (1997): p. 172.

not had clear answers back in July of 1993. Second, for the entire duration of my stay in Japan, I lived in a state of utter confusion and uncertainty. I did not know what was occurring in my immediate surroundings and how it might negatively affect me in a foreign land. Third, I had not had a clear or a graceful exit strategy from Shiseido and Japan in case the employment arrangement did not work out as expected. I simply had an irrationally exuberant and blind faith in the employment arrangement Shiseido had offered me. Fourth, I only had a rudimentary understanding of Japanese social structure and culture. Throughout the 1980's and in the early 1990's, I had heard from various sources and read in the popular media that Japan was making fantastic advancements in business and in its economic conditions. It was often said that by 2000, Japan was to overtake the United States in terms of its GDP size. When I went to Japan, therefore, I thought I was going to Utopia. I was dead wrong.

When I was back in California during the first week of November, 1994, I stayed with my parents for the first two days. On the day after my arrival in California, I was so glad to be back in the U. S. and to see my dog, Hilde, an Akita, that I took her out for a walk in the morning. Hilde was extremely glad to see me, too, and she jumped all over me. She was a big wolf-size dog, and in the confusion, I fell down and hit my rib on the street curb, and I fractured one of my rib bones. As a consequence of this, I could not laugh, get up alone from my bed in the morning, or engage in any kind of rigorous daily task for nearly three months at my parents' house. During that time, for some strange reason, it rained a lot in the Northern California. The weather was very unusual during that time in California, and it was not even identified as *El Niño*. Thus, partly due to the unfortunate accident and partly due to this strange weather, I had to stay at home for a long while, and I was drawn in by the memories of suffering that I had to endure while I was in Japan, and I drifted into a state of mental delirium and confusion for the next several months. And during that time, I decided to file an official complaint against Shiseido for the mistreatment that I received with the U. S. Department of Labor in Washington, D. C.; the U. S. Ambassador to Japan, Walter Mondale; and DISCO company that initially found me an employment with Shiseido back in 1992. I have also sent the copies of the complaint to Shiseido Human Resources Department and the president of Shiseido.

There is plenty of everything in California: Fresh fruits, vegetables, restaurants, computers, movies, flavored coffee, *etc.* I am a lot happier here in California, for I am able to do things that I truly enjoy and cherish in life. I am taking German and French language classes again, and I hope to earn an advanced business degree in a few years. It is a bit of a mystery to this date as to why on earth I chose to go to Japan to live and work. Because I had been discriminated against and suffered so much in New England that I must have been looking for a better and an egalitarian life elsewhere outside the U. S. For the first six months of my stay in Japan, I saw Japan through a pair of rosy spectacles. Although there were plenty of warnings as to how wretched my life might be during that time, I kept on ignoring them. The turning point came one night in January of 1994 when I found myself on a hyper-crowded train with swollen red eyes. The eye conditions developed for working too long and looking into the sunlight in front of a bare window on the sixth floor of the Shiseido Omori International HQ where the only Macintosh computer in the entire building could be found. In this utterly pitiful fix that I found myself in, I asked myself: "How did this happen?" The pivotal role of the Macintosh computer in bringing about the misery is explained in detail in this book. This is a story about how a person dealt with apparent national and cultural differences in a foreign land from a disadvantaged position. There are many lessons to be learned in the story:

A young American President named William Jefferson Clinton had just been elected in 1992 and has recently paid his homage to Japan. He has made passionate speeches throughout his stay in Japan at the Diet, the Tokyo University and other prominent institutions. His visit has galvanized the population in this small island nation that had emerged as the new economic superpower just in the last decade. Some economists had even predicted then that Japan would surpass the U. S. as the new economic giant in the 1990's. By the early 1990's, "internationalization," "globalization" and "cosmopolitan" were the corporate buzzwords in that island nation. The yen was so strong that it was trading at $1.00 per ¥100 in 1993 and 1994.

Originally founded in 1872 as a pharmacy in Ginza, Shiseido is a forward-looking company, which had introduced many Western novelties to Japan. These included Japan's first toothpaste, perfume, soda fountain and color cosmetics. Its founder was a Columbia University graduate and was a die-hard Francophile. Shiseido, Japan's largest cosmetics company, produces makeup and skin care products. It also makes toiletries, professional salon hair care products, pharmaceuticals and fine chemicals. Other interests include a chain of about 45 Ginza fashion boutiques; specialty fragrance, hair and skin care salons, including *Les Salons du Palais Royal* Shiseido fragrance salon in Paris; and a dozen Shiseido Parlour restaurants and food shops. Currently, there are over 25,000 employees around the world working for Shiseido. The company sells its products in more than 50 countries, and although the company had penetrated the entire E. U. market, plus Switzerland and Austria by the fiscal year 1992, about 90% of its entire sales still came from Japan. This was hardly an acceptable figure for a company that wished to pride itself as a global organization. Shiseido was striving to increase international sales to 25% of its total by the fiscal year 2001.[2] At the start of a new decade in 1990, therefore, in order to achieve its international sales goal by 2001, the company sensed a need for a diversification of its work force. "Diversification" in this case was a euphemism for hiring non-Japanese workers; *i. e.,* white Caucasian workers, so it started to aggressively recruit white employees through such employment agency as DISCO. I was a part of this grand diversification scheme. By 1992, there were nearly a dozen non-Japanese foreigners (*"gaijin"*) and Caucasians working for the firm. Because it was a cosmetics company, they were predominantly female employees, and they called themselves affectionately, "Shiseido Girls." Just as the whole world of stage for the Spice Girls was Britain, the whole theater for the Shiseido Girls was Japan. Not unlike the Spice Girls, the Shiseido Girls had a big bang of a start, and they eventually disintegrated and faded away. By 1995, all but one was gone, and there was only a vague part of remaining Japanese worker's fading collective memory. Against this backdrop, I was offered an employment contract from Shiseido for a year in 1992 through DISCO, and from July of 1993 to November of 1994 until I abruptly left Japan, I was put through a tremendous amount of psychological and physical trauma in Tokyo. When a person has undergone a traumatic experience, the person tends to suppress the memory for a long time because it is best to be forgotten. We see this phenomenon quite often amongst the Holocaust survivors, who only recently, after five decades of silence, began to speak up. I regret enormously that I have not written this book earlier, for I had to suppress my memories for the past twelve years.

I have always known subconsciously that these memories had to be let out someday, but I did not see any urgency or need for all these years; that was, until I met Jean-Christian de La Chevalerie once again for the first time after four years of separation at the *Château-Rouge* Station in the *18e arrondissement* in Paris on July 12, 1998. Jean-Christian was a trusted co-worker at the Omori Shiseido International HQ where I used to work. He was the only true friend that I have ever made while I was in Japan. When I returned to California a week later, I embarked on a search for my past, and I began to write like a madman. The time that I had spent in Tokyo constituted a strong foundation of my life, not unlike those college years that I had spent in New England. In Japan, I suffered all the discrimination normally directed against all *gaijin*, but enjoyed none of the privileges reserved for a white Caucasian *gaijin*. At one level, I am very bitter about this painful period of my life, but at another level, as Jean-Christian reminded me, I should be, to a small degree, thankful that I was given an opportunity to experience this

---

[2] - http://www.thestandard.net/companies/company_display/0,1591,41884,00.html

aspect of Japan first-hand. It is no exaggeration to say that I did a lot of growing up in Japan. Partly due to the distance, but mostly due to its humid tropical climate, I have never felt quite at home in Japan, and I missed home enormously when I was in Japan. Furthermore, I missed small things in California: Dogs on the streets, children playing at parks, burritos, jalapeños, strawberries, hazelnut coffee, softball matches, uncensored magazines, fresh salads and low-fat vegetarian Chinese food.

Japan is a small country, and I believe it was no coincidence that I actually ran into someone from Shiseido at the Nakita Airport on my way back to the U. S. in July of 1996 when I was on the business trip. I could not recall his name, but he used to sit right next to me in the International Business Department I section, and he was in charge of the Latin American countries. I believe also that he spoke Spanish fluently. He was on his way to Latin America *via* New York, and he was flying a United Airline flight. He was standing right in front of me at the check-in counter. Naturally, I asked him about Jean-Christian, Anne Neumann, Yael Alkalay, Carolyn Lattin, Mr. Takahashi, Mr. Arai, Mr. Nagai, Mr. Miyazaki, Ms. Shioya, and everyone else. I was told that all the foreign workers eventually quit after my resignation, and there were only two intern workers - one from Australia and the other from France - at the Shiseido Omori International HQ. I was also told that Mr. Miyzaki has been assigned to Shiseido Deutschland; Jean-Christian went back to France; Anne Neumann, Carolyn Lattin, and Yael Alkalay all returned to the U. S. So this book is about the Shiseido Girls, the real Japan and the events that took place 20 year ago in a far away place, an ocean away, in a city so crowded and in a nation whose economic might was only second to that of the United States.

CHAPTER 2

White Supremacy in Japanese Society

If there were two key determinants that could predict a human being's fate on this earth, they had to be the race and gender, but no where on earth, this fact is more profoundly true than in Japan. In Appendices of this book, there are an article titled, "Ethnic Japanese find tightly closed society" from the *San Jose Mercury News,* dated Wednesday, July 30, 1997, reporting on the experience of Luis Adaniya; an article titled, "The Land of Rising Crom," from *SURFER* magazine, written by Chris Cote; an article titled, "Fond Memories of Life with a Host Family," from *MANGAJIN* magazine, written by Peter Shepard; and an article titled, "American Gigolo," from *SWING* magazine, written by Tyler Thoreson. As readers can see, Luis Adaniya reports diametrically different view of Japan from those of Chris Cote, Peter Shepard and Tyler Thoreson. How does one reconcile this? Why is Luis Adaniya's perception of Japan so different from the other three white Caucasian men? How can similar circumstances result in such contrasting experiences? The answer is simple. It is his race. The strong fallacy in the U. S. is that an Asian-American person might fare better in Japan because of the racial commonality. This is absolutely incorrect, and it can not be further from the truth. Because Japan is an openly racist society of a colonial type (*i. e.,* white supremacy), it discriminates against non-whites with even more vengeance, and there exists no active social infrastructure or strong and conscientious social movement to correct this illness. Imagine a nation of Caucasoid-philes where everything a white person does is revered and admired. Make that nation to be the second largest economy in the world. We now have an Asian colony in which Caucasians of all stripes thrive in every corner and fabrics of its society. World War II had an irreversibly profound effect on the collective Japanese psychic. The occupying U. S. forces have done an excellent job in supplanting a Eurocentric society in an Asian nation. Anyone of 7.87 trillion Caucasians around the world, should he or she chooses to be in Japan, would instantly enjoy an elevated status as a privileged first class citizen. This is incredible, yet so true. So the Japanese live out their days, worshiping and imitating Caucasians. For Japanese, gaining an upper hand in every aspect of his or her social, business, career, or academic advancement is to be somehow associated with a white person or a Caucasian institution. So the billboards, advertisements and TV commercials are filled with images of racially-Caucasian entities and written in English, French or German. An ultimate life goal of a hip Japanese woman is to be married to an unattractive Caucasian male and to give birth to a Eurasian baby. So this is done on a wholesale scale. Marriage to a Caucasian is deemed as the quickest and the most instant way to establish one's legitimacy. Likewise, to sell anything in Japan, the product must be associated with a Caucasian image or institution. For example, when Shiseido introduced a new product in the market, it had to come up with a French name; otherwise, I was told that it would not be bought. So Shiseido came up with non-sense French phrases. As long as they "sounded" French, everything would be honky-dory. Since the time of the French-Indian War, things French are looked down upon in New England. This is never the case in Japan. The whole nation is in madly love with France. One would often see store names and signs in French in Tokyo. In the fashionable parts of Tokyo, one would frequently see signs that read, *"On parle français ici."* Japan is an incredible Francophile nation, where the entire populace adores everything French. No one questioned this strangeness. So in this humid and tropical climate, Caucasian fungi of all stripes flourished.

On the day I met Dana Jourdan for the first time in July of 1993, I inquired her forthrightly: "Have you encountered any form of discrimination in Japan?" Her reply was somewhat surprising at the time: "The Japanese never discriminate against the Caucasians." "They do, however, vigorously discriminate against fellow Asians and blacks." I dismissed her statement. In my naïveté, I did not want to believe it, so I denied it for the first four months. She had reminded me earlier that day in front of Jean-Christian de La Chevalerie that because I did not "look" like him I had to be extra careful and more observant of the Japanese customs and rituals. Again, I dismissed that statement, too, for I did not want believe it. But ultimately she was correct. I should have known better. After all, she was a Japonology major who had spent many years in Japan. She was simply being truthful and courteous to a newcomer from America.

So the unscrupulous riff-raffs from Australia, Britain, Canada, France, New Zealand and the U. S. enjoyed their elevated status as privileged beings in Japan. But it did not stop there. Due to the strong yen in 1993, adventurers from Brazil, Columbia, Israel, Iran, Russia, Scandinavia and Spain enjoyed instant qualification to become "high fashion" models in Japan. Aware of suddenly elevated status, some of them actually became Japanophiles themselves. At home, they were nobody, but in Japan, they immediately realized that they were privileged beings. Examples of this phenomenon are detailed below under *White Women in Japan.* At soap houses, or brothels, Latin American women were promoted as "Nordic" beauties. As long as they appeared racially-Caucasian, it did not make any difference in Japan. (*Vide* Appendices)

The Japanese language reflected this ridiculous racial paradigm. Since the time of the U. S. occupation, the term "American" has come to be synonymous with Caucasian. So one was considered and called an "American," even if the person was in reality from Kosovo, South Africa or Cuba, so long as the person was racially-qualified to be Caucasoid. The language lacked the proper terminology to describe the complexities and diversity of the ethno-linguistic reality of the world. In the Japanese universe, one was either Japanese or "American," and there was no other. It was somewhat similar to the German term, *der Ausländer.* In the strictest legal sense, anyone that did not hold a Japanese passport was a *gaijin*, yet in the Japanese colloquial understanding, *only* the Caucasians were considered foreigners or *gaijin.* Just as the Germans understood *die Ausländers* in multi-tiers,[3] so did the Japanese. In the Japanese cosmos, there were at least three distinct tiers of *gaijin.* The upper tier was comprised of white Americans, Australians, Canadians, Europeans and anyone with fair complexion. The Japanese regarded these groups of people with reverence and admiration. The Japanese *never* discriminate against the people that belonged to this upper tier. The middle tier was made up of assimilated Koreans, Chinese and people from other Asian countries. The Japanese tended to have neutral or slightly negative attitudes towards these groups of people. Discrimination was practiced against the people from this tier only when the circumstances permitted, or it was convenient, necessary, unchallenged or known to have no negative consequences. It was the *gaijin* that belonged to the third bottom tier that experienced the most fierce level of discrimination from the Japanese. Unassimilated Asians, African-, Asian-, Latino-Americans, the people from the Middle East, Latin America and Africa would belong to this tier. Archaically, the term, *gaijin,* used to only refer to the people from the first tier. During a new product line introduction conference held by Shiseido in March of 1994, for example, only *gaijin* models were used. This meant

---

[3] - Thränhardt. Dietrich. "Patterns of organization among different ethnic minorities." *New German Critique.* (1989): pp. 10-26.

that there were no black models. All models were Caucasians, except one Asian.

In the summer of 1993, into this racially-objectified abstract universe, I was let in, and the people around me could not reconcile the apparent contradiction that I displayed. Thus, the likes of Messrs. Kanda, Arai and Oscar Godoy had to justify their core prejudices and release their irritations and frustrations on me for creating vulnerability to their core beliefs. Sufficed to say, I was their walking antithesis that constantly reminded them of the false premises in the Japanese racial paradigm. I challenged the validity of the two separate and distinct spheres in their dichotomy. A perfect example was the following event:

On June 22, 1994, on or about 3:30 PM, on the sixth floor of the Shiseido Omori International HQ building at room 605, when the team from the Overseas Trademark Section of the Patent Department paid a visit for Messrs. Sarraf and Nazjarian of CH Sarraf & Co. from Lebanon, we were seated face-to-face with the members of the Patent Department for a conference. The visiting members were comprised of Messrs. Ryozo Mori, General Manager; Shiro Emori, Deputy General Manager; Akira Seki; Messes. Yoko Doi; Diane Hase; and Mimi Gumelaty.

When Mr. T. Arai proceeded to introduce the International Business Department II staff members, which included Messrs. Sugita, Kimura, de La Chevalerie, he stated names, positions and duties. He identified Jean-Christian de La Chevalerie as being a "French." When it was my turn to be introduced, I was identified as being an "American" from "San Francisco." Upon this introduction, Mr. Mori promptly retorted, "Are you a Japanese American?" When I replied "No," he immediately countered, "Humm, 'Parker,' huh? What is your ancestry?" After this question a long silence ensued. During this soundless state, I had to search for the most proper and appropriate term for reply. This demand for identification of ancestry was expressed in the most awkward setting in front of visiting guests from overseas for a maximum embarrassment effect.

I keenly noted that Mr. Mori bothered not to inquire Jean-Christian, who happened to be white, but of a Belgian background, of his ancestry. In order to exacerbate the situation, when the group adjourned for a break, Ms. Doi proceeded to humiliate me by prompting a non-sense question as to "whether I spoke the Korean language." When I replied as to why she should have a need to know

21

whether I spoke Korean or not, she returned this sardonic answer: "My department is experiencing a 'problem' with lawyers from Korea."

In order not to stage an open confrontation in front of the visitors, I politely stated that I knew nothing of that language.

Needless to say, this episode was racially charged. It was clearly demonstrated by the fact that Jean-Christian was never placed under the same scrutiny and embarrassment by the virtue of his white race. In terms of the historical precedence, I felt like a Jew in the 1930's Germany, as I was so thoroughly racially scrutinized and questioned. The public identification process is the most rudimentary, the rawest, and the crucial step toward persecution and discrimination. If there is no need to discriminate, there certainly is no need for any identification. It must be noted that in this particular racial offense, Mr. Mori did not ask Jean-Christian of his ancestry, nor did Ms. Doi ask Jean-Christian "whether he spoke Korean."

When I think of Japan now, I conjure up the filth of Tokyo crowds and the unbearable humidity. I have never seen or been aware of the picturesque and romantically snow-covered Mount Fuji accentuated by a dash of the super modern bullet train at its hills, or mystic dark temples in Kyoto showered with full blossoms of cherry blossom flower pedals at their spring peak. These are the tourist images of Japan. My recollection of Japan is epitomized by the smell of burning fish. This odor was omnipresent in Japan. My understating of Japan consists of destitute in the midst of opulence, beguiling politeness amid shouting chaos and the smell of burning fish among the mind-numbing skyscrapers.

Life in Japan was not easy. One must purchase a telephone bond from the Nippon Telephone and Telecommunications (NTT) before one could have a telephone line installed to the place of residence. This telephone bond was whopping $800! So I lived without a telephone during my entire stay in Japan. There were no jalapeños found anywhere in Tokyo. Strawberries or any other fresh fruits were over $20 for a small basket. Although Starbucks recently opened its first store in Ginza, flavored coffee in the early the 1990's was non-existent. Tickets at movie theaters were $18. If smoking had been originally popular among the African or Asian cultures, it probably would not have displayed the same explosive popularity that has swept through Japan, but the aggressive advertising campaigns from the U. S. cigarette companies in the 1950's, -60's, -70's and -80's have succeeded in creating a quintessential Japanese axiom that smoking equals being Caucasian. So it was everywhere, and their ads run openly even on TV. The government took no action to curve this crime against the humanity. Never mind that smoking caused cancer. If it was white man's cancer, it must be a good cancer. Moreover, the concepts of public health and nutrition did not seem to exist in Japan. High consumption of red meat accompanied by high caloric and cholesterol was still considered "healthy." Everywhere in Japan, meat, eggs and peanuts were falsely advertised as parts of a potent "high energy" meal. It was an incredibly meat loving society. There will come a time in two decades or so when a record number of the Japanese begin to die of throat and lung cancer, heart diseases and strokes. The Japanese government should take a note: An ounce of prevention is worth a pound of cure.

Japan is an industrialized nation of farmers. It is an agricultural society trapped in a body of an economic giant. As has been said many times before, Japan has a collectivist culture. Collectivists cultures are rooted in social groups; individuals are viewed as members of groups. Furthermore, people of collectivist cultures view their work groups and organizations as a fundamental part of themselves. [4] Thus, when introduced, one always identifies oneself by saying, "I am Jane Smith of Company X," or "I am John Doe of Y University" in Japan. I had been well aware of the theory, but I had not understood the theoretical application of this concept in daily life. It was precisely this cultural view of an individual as a member of a group actively fostered the racist climate in Japan. The penalty for not knowing the theoretical application of this collectivist concept in daily life could be extremely serious. I made a serious *faux pas* when I decided not to attend a wedding of a co-worker in my department at Shiseido once. I have heard from someone that guests had to bring money or make donations, usually ¥30,000,[5] at Japanese weddings. The number "30,000" was normally picked because the number had to be an odd number for indivisibility at the wedding, and "10,000" would be too small for a donation. So my logic was not to attend: Dinner at the Shiseido Nippacho *Mes Amis* dormitory was free, and I needed not listen to the long and boring speeches that usually accompanied at a Japanese wedding. This turned out to be a major social offense, for everyone, including Anne Neumann and Jean-Christian de La Chevalerie, attended the wedding, except me. No one mentioned about this incident at the office, so I did not think of it much at the beginning, but my myopia to save ¥30,000 resulted in my being labeled as a maverick for the rest of my stay in Japan. In a collectivist culture, the group (family, tribe, team or in this case the International Business Department II) is the center of attention, and

---

[4] - Thompson, Leigh L. *The Mind and Heart of the Negotiator.* Upper Saddle River, NJ: Prentice Hall. (1998): p. 286.
[5] - ¥100 ~ $1 in 1993 and 1994.

individual behavior gets attention only if it deviates from group norms.[6] And my behavior of not attending the wedding deviated from the group norm in a fantastic way. I hoped that someone would have warned me about this beforehand. It was clearly my ignorance in intercultural social skills.

Japan is an industrialized nation of farmers, and Japanese social groups still function as though they were in a farming community. An example of this was the concept of the community chest. Whenever there was a wedding, death, earthquake, or serious illness somewhere, employees were expected to contribute money for an *ad hoc* relief fund. So I was expected to make "voluntary" donations at least once a month to a wedding, disaster or funeral, of which I had absolutely no knowledge because someone was always passing around an envelope for donations at the Shiseido Omori International HQ. These donations added up to ¥150,000 in a year. These would make a perfect sense for the Japanese employees because the collectivist culture dictated that all the donations they made would eventually be returned to them when it was their turn to get married, their parents who passed away or their family members that were suffering from the effects of a typhoon. Collectivists tend to be concerned about the results of their actions on members of in-group, share resources with in-group members, feel interdependent with in-groups members and feel involved in the lives of the in-groups members.[7] To me, however, this phenomenon amounted to nothing, but taxation without representation.

A community chest also existed at the company housing, the Shiseido Nippacho *Mes Amis* dormitory, and I was expected to pay my share. I resisted, however, because no other *gaijin* worker at Shiseido was required to pay such a share because none of them was arranged to live at a company housing. One can almost claim that this was an overt form of discrimination because I was placed at the company housing simply based on my race and gender with other Japanese employees, and therefore, I had to pay unnecessary expenses. Expressed differently, my contribution to the community chest at the company housing was tantamount to penalty for not being a white Caucasian *gaijin* employee. I could not understand why the Shiseido HR Department did not see it the same way. This topic is described further below under *Hidden Penalties for Living at the Shiseido Nippacho* Mes Amis *Dormitory*. Incidentally, no such hidden expenses and the cost of installing a telephone line (¥85,000) were mentioned in the employment

---

[6] - *Ibid.*, Cook, Hunsaker and Coffey, p. 206.

[7] - Hui, C. Harry and Harry C. Triandis, Harry C. "Individualism-collectivism: A study of cross-cultural researchers." *Journal of Cultural Psychology.* 17 (1986): pp. 225-248.

contract given to me by the Shiseido HR Department before I had gone to Japan (*Vide* Appendices).

President Kennedy Speech

In Japan, newcomers are often asked to embarrass themselves by giving speeches of introduction at public meetings. Such an opportunity came to me one day in September of 1993 at a monthly division-wide morning meeting. With a large black microphone in my hand, I gave an eloquent speech in front of 150 or so employees at the Shiseido Omori International HQ. The speech was carefully scripted a few weeks before, as I had once already botched a similar speech of introduction at the HR Department in Ginza. So I typed out a speech and memorized it. New employees and transfers were introduced in the order of seniority, and these introductions tended to be very formal. Men usually fixed their ties and shirts and wore jackets. I was the third one to be introduced. I did not know all this, so I delivered a perfect speech with my necktie loose and my shirt sleeves up to an audience of bewildered employees:

"Good morning. My name is Pierce Parker. Please call me Pierce. I would like to apologize for speaking in English, but in order to convey a precise message from the bottom of my heart, I think it is necessary. I have come a long way across an ocean to your country, and I would like to believe that I came with a specific mission.

My mission here is to create a synergy. Synergy is a term in chemistry whereby two independent elements combined together creating a devastating force. So the synergy between your Japanese management style and my American background would create such a powerful force that no one would be able to stop us. I have already learned a lot about management in your country, and in closing I would like to paraphrase that famous speech by President Kennedy: 'Ask not what your company can do for you, but ask what you can do for your company.' Thank you."

No one applauded. In the audience was the executive vice president of the International HQ. Mr. Nagai stood up immediately after me and did an instant translation of my speech. I did not think much of this event afterward, but I began to notice that other employees started to treat me nicer and seemed to smile at me more. In a way, this was my defining moment of big bang start at Shiseido. Soon a lot of ebullient employees commented that my speech was just like the ones given by President Clinton only a few weeks ago and was very "American" thing to do. I could count at least five people in my memory who praised me for the speech. So I was very happy for the time being, not knowing what was in store for my future life in Japan. I had a euphoric sense of forward momentum, for I was given a new lease in life. I was about to make it big in Japan. For that brief period, I was the most optimistic person in Japan. I only spoke of a bright and rosy future in Japan with others. This was about to change very quickly.

CHAPTER 3

July 12, 1998
Saturday, 11:00 AM, Sunny and Mild
18e Arrondissement in Paris
At a *Café* near *Le Sacré Cœur* and *Square Willette*

France has just won the World Cup, and Bastille Day was only two days away. Children were blasting firecrackers, and the noise from the constant explosions was causing headaches. Despite the noise, the conversation had to continue. For the topic of the conversation took Jean-Christian de La Chevalerie and me to another place far way and another time a long, long ago. It was a fact-finding conversation both of us were dying to have for the past four years. This day had to happen some day. For years, I had dreamed about it and formulated the exact topics for it, but when the actual event took place, it was all free-floating. Those sitting around us probably wondered what these two men were shouting back and forth amid the excruciating noise. None would ever guess that it was exactly five years ago in downtown Tokyo where Jean-Christian and I had first met. Both of us were very young and naïve then. We met at a conference room in Shibuya in early morning. We both had to attend a week-long seminar and learn about the Japanese society, history, business practices, economy and people at the Japan Productivity Center on the north side of the Shibuya Station. Also at the conference table were Cameron Brown and Anne Neumann. Being so eager and excited about my new life in Tokyo, I never paid close attention to their presence, demeanor, nor did I have any clairvoyance as to what was to come for the next 15 months. Looking back, I was simply too eager and optimistic about my new life in Tokyo and overlooked some crucial signs and indications. It took me nearly six months to realize that I had made a terrible mistake of coming to Tokyo to work for Shiseido, and by then it was too late. For the next 15 months, I was to meet Messrs. Nagai, Takahashi, Arai, Sugiyama, Kanda; Carolyn Lattin, Dr. Tatsuya Ozawa and Oscar Godoy.

July 20, 1993 Tuesday Overcast and Humid
Shiseido Nippacho *Mes Amis* Dormitory, Yokohama, Japan

It must have been a strange twist of fate, and to this date I resent immensely that the Shiseido HR Department had decided to put me into the company dormitory at Nippacho in Shin-Yokohama Kita in Kanagawa Prefecture. For one, from the Shin-Yokohama Kita Station to the Omori Station, where the Shiseido International Headquarters was located, it was an hour commute door-to-door on two separate, hyper-crowded train lines. For another, it was located in such a remote area that there were virtually no shops, stores or restaurants open after 6 PM or on weekends. While it was conveniently located near the Shiseido Nippacho Research Laboratory Center and was ideal for those Ph.D.'s that were working there, it could not have been any worse for my accommodation. For the implication of living at the Shiseido Nippacho *Mes Amis* dormitory has been far greater than a simple commuting inconvenience and the distance, had I not been assigned to this company housing, my impression of Shiseido, Tokyo and Japan would have been dramatically different. Because I had to live at this company dormitory, my grotesquely negative understanding of the Japanese society began to take shape. It must have been a fate.

Mr. Yukihara Kanda was a diminutive family man with two children, wife and a German Shepherd. He was the resident director of the Shiseido Nippacho *Mes Amis* dormitory and was the undisputed king of his castle. He was empowered with unlimited discretionary power from the Shiseido HR Department, and when such an absolute power, absence of checks and balances and hick ignorance were vested in a provincial man, it was a deadly formula for trouble. He took more than a casual avuncular interest in my life. Mr. Kanda, for all practical purposes, was my moral conduct police, controlling every aspect of my life. Mr. Kanda was absolutely convinced that I was "Korean," and he already had a set of solutions and policies to deal with the "Koreans." For some reason, Mr. Kanda has determined that everything that I had done was because I was "Korean." He used to remind me whenever it snowed, in "my mother's country (Korea)," it would snow a lot more treacherously. He never explicitly said it, but my psychoanalysis skills were good enough to guess that he rationalized his barbarism on the fact that I was a "Korean," and it was acceptable because it was expected that a "Korean" person misbehaved in everything he did in Japan. If there was a fire alarm going off accidentally, there was no need for investigation: That "Korean" person must have set it off. If rainwater dripped into the bathroom through the open window, there was no question as to who kept the window unlocked overnight: It was that "Korean" man. The fact was that I never was a "Korean," but this was irrelevant: In his mind, I was one. If there ever was such thing as a bellicose Japanese redneck, he was it. No amount of scientific evidence or rational thinking would topple his prejudiced reality. He possessed a grotesque disregard for my human and civil rights. This irreducible man was absolutely convinced that his survival was directly correlated to my failure. It must have been beyond extraterrestrial to Mr. Kanda that I was a teetotaler, non-smoker and a vegetarian. He was, in every sense of the word, my exact antithesis. His top priority in improving the lives of the residents at the dormitory was to install cigarette and beer vending machines, not a milk or orange juice vending machine. He did his daily best to make my stay at the Shiseido Nippacho *Mes Amis* dormitory as miserable, uncomfortable and inhabitable as possible. Whenever I think of an evil and intolerant Japanese person today, I picture Mr. Kanda. He was a chain-smoker whose paradigm differed so dramatically from mine, yet he had all the power in the Japanese universe to oppress me and make my life a living hell. I dreaded encountering him on Saturdays and Sundays because he always had something bad to scorn me about, real or imagined. In his Japonocentric universe, I was like an insect that was causing all the troubles and irritations at this dormitory and I had to be crushed. If I had never met him, my understanding and memories of Japan would have been dramatically favorable. I was screamed and yelled at almost every weekend by Mr. Kanda for everything I did. He would get upset over my forgetting to pick up the clean laundry in the laundry room; bringing out the garbage a few hours before the designated time on Mondays; leaving bread crumbs on the table in the cafeteria; not turning off the lights in the bathroom; leaving the windows open in the bathroom; not unplugging the electric cord after using the microwave oven; wandering around the dormitory in shorts thereby committing "sexual" harassment against the female residents; forgetting things in the common area such as cups and magazines; closing the curtains at the cafeteria without his permission; *etc.* In other words, he used to get upset over everything and anything that I did. I remember distinctively that he used to deliberately close the windows in the bathroom during the summer months even when I was inside the bathroom so that I would suffocate with the smell of poignant ammonia and humidity. He used to post large hand written signs all over the bathroom and the kitchen to remind me what I was doing something wrong. He used to lock up the TV room just so that I would not be able to watch TV because if I had been in the TV room, I would allegedly mess up the room. All I used to do was to pull the *kotatsu* near the TV. Thanks to his maliciousness, I have had absolutely no entertainment, no telephone, no TV, no friends, no freedom and no respect. It was no accident that I wished to leave Japan quickly and never go back there ever again.

CHAPTER 4

Hidden Penalties
For Living at the Shiseido
Nippacho *Mes Amis* Dormitory

To Mr. Kanda, my mere presence at Shiseido Nippacho *Mes Amis* dormitory symbolized the declining living standard of Japan and was the sign of social decay. To him, I was the very embodiment of everything that was wrong with Japan. Not unlike what Jean-Marie Le Pen might say in France, Mr. Kanda might contend that non-white migrant worker like myself was rotting the core of his nation. I had to be crushed, so he did his everyday best. Because I was a *gaijin*, I had no family to go back to during the August summer recess or Christmas/New Year's break, so I remained at the Shiseido Nippacho *Mes Amis* dormitory. During those company holiday periods, the cafeteria was also closed. This meant that I had to eat out breakfast, lunch and dinner everyday. I begged for Mr. Kanda's permission to let me cook light meals at the dormitory kitchen, but he flatly denied my request, citing that I would start a fire and burn down the dormitory! So I suffered. I either skipped meals or had to travel to the Shin-Yokohama Station to buy expensive meals at restaurants. Thus, it was no wonder that I came to dislike company holiday periods. I had no access to a TV; I often had to go a great length of trouble to eat; I had no friends and no social life; and I had no telephone. I was very lonely in a strange land. I was forced to into a painstaking existence.

Perhaps the most severe penalty that I had to endure financially by having been required to live at the Shiseido Nippacho *Mes Amis* dormitory was that there was a community chest for emergencies, and every resident was asked to contribute to it "voluntarily." I did not see the need for this community chest, and since it was voluntary, I decided not to pay at the beginning. Why should I pay, I reasoned, when it was tantamount to a fine for not being a white Caucasian employee? After all, no other Caucasian employee had to live in a company dormitory and had to contribute any money "voluntarily." Then why should I? This naturally irritated Mr. Kanda and the leader of the residence council. So the president of the resident council paid a little visit to my room on one Saturday. He reminded me of a New York Mafia debt collector, and he probably thought that he was doing the right thing, not realizing the greater implication of the systematic discriminatory practice he was engaged in. I was taken back, and I did not think he would understand my argument for not paying, so I coughed up $100[8] he demanded, but I made a sharp entry in my racial discrimination mental bank account book: Anne Neumann, Carolyn Lattin or Jean-Christian de La Chevalerie never had to pay any fine for being Caucasian employees. It was not about the money. It was about the inequality. The perception of inequality was becoming a major threat to the continuance of my relationship with the Shiseido Company.

If Mr. Kanda had been a white American, he would have been a good church-going, God-fearing, family man. This was 1993, not 1953, but his moral uprightness explicitly prohibited any overnight guests at the dormitory. It was inconceivable in his tiny Puritanical moral set that anyone would engage in any sexual acts before marriage, or so he wished to project his moral portrait to the company and to the Ph.D. residents in their 20's and 30's at the Shiseido Nippacho *Mes Amis* dormitory. He must have had a few Chihuahuas of his own in his youth, but never mind that: No overnight guest meant no premarital sex. So the residents had to go to love hotels in Yokohama and Shin-Yokohama with their girlfriends, having to waste up to $1,000 for a weekend from their meager salaries that they earned. Such feeble-mindedness of Mr. Kanda cost the residents there tens of thousands of dollars each year, yet no one challenged his moral supremacy. Not that I had any interest in testing the legality of Mr. Kanda's moral prohibition, but that I was very much amused by his hypercritical ignorance and backwardness. So I asked him once point-blank, when I was forced to go drinking with him at a nearby eatery, as to why he would not allow any overnight guests. He righteously replied that it was because he was not running a "love hotel" at the Shiseido Nippacho *Mes Amis* dormitory. What a simpleton he was, I thought. His slightly higher grasp of the reality would have made his residents so much happier, saved so much money and bring about healthier outlooks in life. I had to excuse myself from the table immediately after hearing his answer because I was about to regurgitate the barbecued sparrow morsel I was coerced to taste. Mr. Kanda must have forgotten in his drunkenness that I was a vegetarian, but I played along with him in order not

---

[8] - ¥100 ~ $1 in 1993 and 1994.

to provoke him too much. I went back directly to my dorm room. Mr. Kanda's moral prohibition did not matter to me anyway. I had no one to bring back to my dorm room as an overnight guest, and even if I had someone, no sane woman would travel an hour to come to Nippacho in Kanagawa Prefecture just to spend a night under the hawky prison guard gazes of Mr. Kanda. His moral prohibition did matter on one level, however, and it did register sharply in my racial discrimination awareness mental bank account book: Anne Neumann and other Caucasian employees never had to live under this prohibition, and they could bring anyone they wished to their places of residence as overnight guests. I was certain that Mr. Kanda thought he was doing the right thing, not realizing the greater implication of the discriminatory practice he was engaged in, so I dared not challenge his prohibition. In Mr. Kanda's universe, his prohibition on overnight guests absolutely prevented promiscuity and premarital sex of the residents.

Behavior Report

Adding to my misery index, one of the omnipotent authorities that Mr. Kanda was empowered with was the "behavior report," which was directly submitted to the Shiseido HR Department. On this report, Mr. Kanda was free to write any abnormality he felt proper to document. Although I never saw the report first-hand, I was told from Ms. Ishiwata at the Shiseido HR Department when my annual contract was to be renewed, that my violations at the Shiseido Nippacho *Mes Amis* dormitory included eating too much at the dormitory cafeteria and keeping my windows not shut in my room.

The dormitory itself was consisted of two buildings. The Kandas lived on the first floor next to the entrance. Many of the 90 or so residents held Ph.D. in various scientific disciplines. Almost all worked at the nearby Shiseido Nippacho Research Laboratory Center, which was only five minutes on foot. I was one of five residents that did not work there. There was a small lobby area with an elevator and the cafeteria. The food service at the cafeteria was exclusively for the Japanese residents. Although it was well-prepared and presented, there were no vegetarian *entrées*. There were no cereals, fresh fruits, toasts, coffee or tea for breakfast. While having Japanese food for dinner for over a year was tolerable, having it for breakfast for so long was an entirely different matter. The breakfast was usually consisted of rice and burned fish. There also was a small mail room where packages, shirts and other items from a dry cleaner were kept before they were picked up by the residents. The dormitory still had the smell of fresh paint when I arrived there in July of 1993. Apparently, Shiseido Company owned a lot of properties in the Nippacho neighborhood. The Shin-Yokohama Kita Station was decorated with a wall sculpture financed by Shiseido. Mr. Nagai once told me that he himself had once lived there. He recapped a story of his youth when he and his dorm mates used to eat, drink and bath together at the Shiseido Nippacho *Mes Amis* dormitory. By the time I arrived there in the summer of 1993, however, there was no communal bath. There were two buildings facing each other with multi-level parking lot in the middle. One building, the one with the main entrance on the first floor, obviously was the newer of the two. It had hotel style rooms with individual bathrooms and kitchenettes. The old building had bathrooms and toilets on each floor. I was assigned in the old building. It had no central air-conditioning or heating system, so each room was equipped with an air conditioner for humid summer days and a small boiler in the toilet room to heat up the water for the cold winter days. It was reminiscent of college dormitory, except that in the winter, it was cold and annoying having to wait until the water heated up for several minutes to use. In the summer, it was even worse. It did not register in my mind until the second summer, but the heat and the humidity exacerbated the suffocating odor of ammonia from urine, and the toilet room was infested with mosquitoes and cockroaches. Moreover, because the toilet room was directly facing the Kandas' residence on the first floor, my opening any window for ventilation would immediately prompt Mr. Kanda to dash up to the toilet room and close the windows. Even during the scorching heat and humidity in the summer, Mr. Kanda's concentration camp rule dictated that all windows had to be shut at all times. Otherwise, he would reason that raindrops would come in. Ironically, his real "enemies" were Anne Neumann, Carolyn Lattin and Jean-Christian de La Chevalerie, but they were not required to reside at the Shiseido Nippacho *Mes Amis* dormitory by the Shiseido HR Department and were kept away from his prison guard gaze, and thus I became his resident pet trouble-maker to be toyed with on a daily basis.

Trash Day

The residents at the Shiseido Nippacho *Mes Amis* dormitory were absolutely required by Mr. Kanda to dispose their rubbish between 7 AM and 8 AM sharp on Mondays. Any violator of this rule would be severely scolded and reprimanded by Mr. Kanda. One Sunday after I returned from a business trip to Istanbul, I knew that I would not be able to wake up next morning in time to throw away my trash - and I had accumulated quite a bit - so I took it out the night before. This naturally enraged Mr. Kanda. The rubbish had to have come from that "Korean" man because it contained, amongst other unusual items, Swedish and Israeli fashion magazines. I was scorned and yelled at severely. No doubt Mr. Kanda duly recorded this transgression of mine on my behavior report.

TV Room

On the second floor of the old building, there was a large TV room. It was furnished with *tatamis,* a square table, *kotatsu,* and sitting mats. During the first few weekends after my arrival at the Shiseido Nippacho *Mes Amis* dormitory in the summer of 1993, I would go there and watch the TV. I enjoyed watching the Japanese TV programs, and it was an excellent way to learn the language. On one Friday in August of 1993, however, I discovered that the TV room was locked up. I knew instantly that Mr. Kanda has locked it up so as to prevent me from going inside. I was very circumspect and dared not to bring up the issue at all with Mr. Kanda, but I knew he would argue that I was messing up the TV room by placing the *kotatsu* table too close to the TV. I was not used to sitting on the *tatami* floor, so I sat on the *kotatsu* table whenever I was watching the TV. Thus my only source of entertainment at the Shiseido Nippacho *Mes Amis* dormitory was single-highhandedly eliminated. There was no enjoyment to come home to at the end of stressful work day at the office and the horrifically crowded commute. Mr. Kanda was incredibly kind and generous man indeed.

The Shiseido Nippacho *Mes Amis* Dormitory Layout *

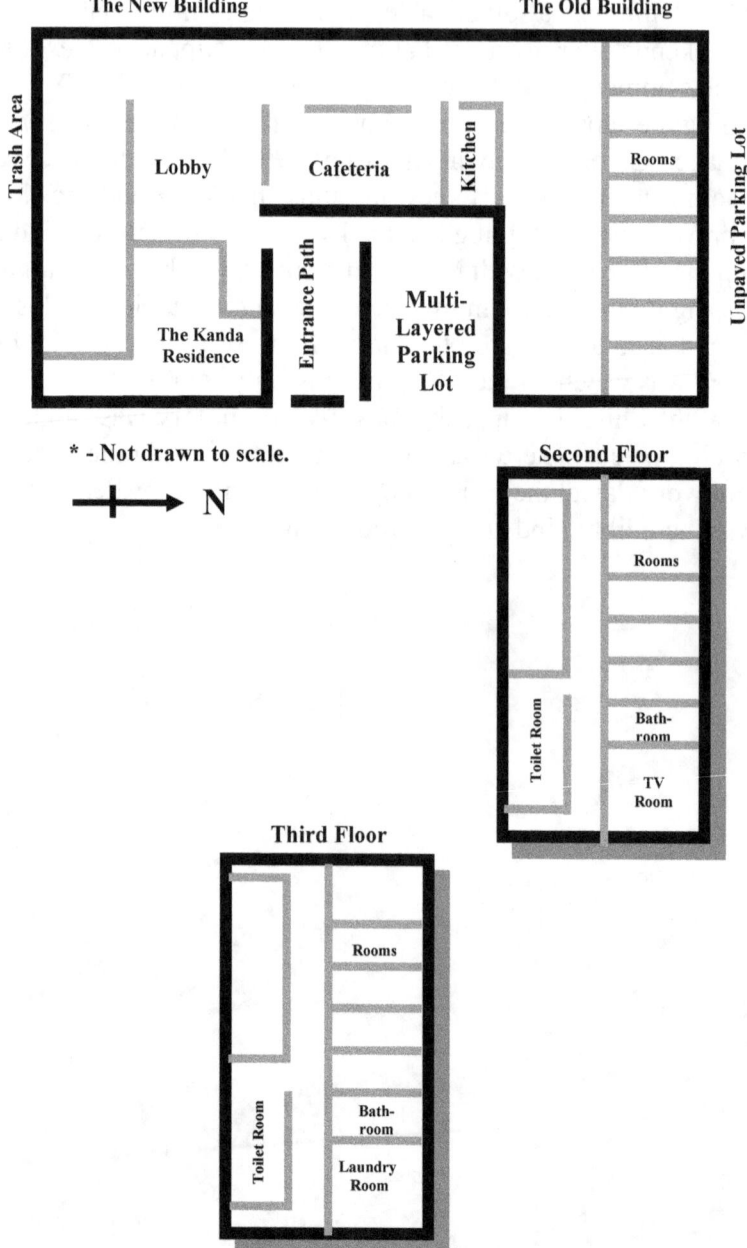

* - Not drawn to scale.

CHAPTER 5

Oscar Godoy

Oscar Godoy was the most curious creature that I met in Japan. Although I inquired about extensively, no one exactly knew any details of this man. Oscar was a Hispano-Caucasian man in his late 40's or early 50's who held English classes at the Shiseido Nippacho Research Laboratory Center once a week. I was initially introduced to Oscar through Dr. Takahiko Suwa when I was searching for a used Macintosh computer. Oscar spoke with heavy English accents, and I suspected that he grew up somewhere in England. I was once told that he befriended Dr. Tatsuya Ozawa, the head of the Shiseido Nippacho Research Laboratory Center, in his youth and was hired by Shiseido to teach English to Ph.D.'s and prepare them to take whatever the English language exams that the Shiseido researchers had to take to go abroad. Oscar had been with Shiseido for over 20 years, and in essence he was running an enterprise of his own within this giant international corporation as a sub-business unit. He lived somewhere in Kamakura, the Beverly Hills of Japan, and he drove the latest Volvo family sedan. Mysteriously, all his wealth was padded from the meager salary that he was receiving as a part-time English teacher at the Shiseido Nippacho Research Laboratory Center. Even more mysterious still, his name was not listed in the phone directory, which was extremely unorthodox in an open society that was Japan. Nor was his Volvo registered in his name with the Japanese Department of Motor Vehicle (DMV). He had a brother who lived in one of the most exclusive neighborhoods of Tokyo where foreign diplomats and ambassadors resided. No one at the Shiseido Nippacho *Mes Amis* dormitory ever visited or knew the exact home address of Oscar in Kamakura. He had absolutely no interaction with his students outside the classroom, which was also extremely unusual in Japan. Before I returned home in November of 1994, I searched the public records extensively about

Oscar Godoy's whereabouts and particulars in Japan. Foolish and subservient Japanese civil servants seemed to believe that protecting a Caucasian man's privacy, no matter how horrific and evil crimes he might have committed, was a civic virtue and a national obligation. It was in this Caucasian love-prejudiced Japanese society that Oscar Godoy has come to flourish for 20 years, and however unscrupulous he might have been, he was above any government persecution or civil litigation. It was only in this illiquid, closed and hush-hush Japanese society that he has come to master the inner workings of the people and their gullible mindset. Oscar Godoy was a *profiteer extraordinaire* whose existence was conceivable only in Asia. Within himself, he knew well that he was a small time Mafia thug with little education, but from without and from the eyes of the Japanese society, he was a highly-educated, polished and sophisticated English "gentleman." His race, gender and accents were the indisputable proofs. Furthermore, he must have learned sometime ago the usefulness of hiding his home address in Japan in conducting his unscrupulous daily affairs. In this small insular nation, where non-confrontational stance was a social virtue, hiding home address meant warding off 99% of his potential troubles instantly. Little did he know that I would eventually constitute the remaining 1% in the most memorable way.

Apple Macintosh Computer Scandal

This might be difficult for readers to believe, but in 1993, the employees were still using pen and paper to conduct daily operations at Shiseido. What I attempted to do at the Shiseido; that is, to bring the Apple computer technology to Shiseido, was a very noble concept. I had absolutely nothing to gain personally. The Shiseido employees will use the softwares that I introduced to Shiseido - Adobe Illustrator, Photoshop, PageMaker, Persuasions (now Power Point), Microsoft Word, Excel, *etc.* - for the generations to come in the future. I was simply trying to modernize the company, but because of the characters like Mr. Arai and Oscar Godoy, my attempt was grossly criticized, impeded and rebuffed, and it also served as the foundation of my unpleasant memories of Japan. I am certain that by now Mr. Nagai, Mr. Takahashi, Ms. Shioya and all others realize that they were making a terrible mistake in not appreciating my noble efforts more in the summer and fall of 1993. If there ever was a legacy about me at Shiseido, I wished it to be remembered as the young American man that brought modern computerization and window-based desktop computing technology to its international headquarters in 1993. Because it was a consensus-based collectivist system at the Shiseido in particular and in the Japanese society in general, no one had initiated to bring an Apple Macintosh computer to the office although the technology had been around for over a decade by 1993. Such a "transgression" would be seen as an act of a maverick and being too uppity and arrogant. Like many firms in Japan, Shiseido was a highly structured organization that valued conformity. In such an organization, initiative was frowned upon and even penalized. Therefore, the collectivist corporate culture at Shiseido has been stifling a swift innovation in office computerization. I had never imagined in my wildest dreams that some day I would become a missionary for computer technology in, of all the countries around the world, the high technology Mecca of Japan. Yet such was the fate I found myself in.

To this suffocating, pretentious, authoritarian and closed office I was let in one day in July of 1993. It was literally a white-collar sweat shop: Some 150 workers shared two typewriters, which no one used in reality, four fax machines and three copy machines. At the International Business Department II, there were three PC laptop computers. One was exclusively for Anne Neumann, and the rest of ten or so people shared the other two. There was no LAN, let alone any computer connections of any kind. I observed Anne Neumann many times, having to bring her laptop to the only printer, make connections with a cable and make printouts. She was still using DOS-based WordPerfect from the late 1980's. There was no central computer data router or server. In my naïveté, I believed throughout the first month in August of 1993 that there was a large computer lab hidden somewhere on a different floor, equipped with the state-of-the-art hardware and software. I held onto the belief that I was not led to it because I was still a new employee, and the company needed to protect its trade secrets. I was dead wrong.

One morning in September of 1993, Mr. Nagai requested me to write a letter. It was a simple one-page letter without any technical details, yet without MS Word, it took me nearly an hour correcting spelling mistakes, adjusting margins and retyping it to perfection. I asked Mr. Nagai and the others where they kept the Apple Macintoshes. They nervously laughed and giggled. This was my first encounter with that famous Japanese nervous laughter.

It was this unwillingness to respond swiftly to my inquiry that the history ought to recognize it as the Japanese brand of racism. If it had been Anne Neumann who made the same inquiry; that is to say, if it had been a Caucasian employee who made the same inquiry, the company would have been extremely eager to please her and accommodate whatever office needs she had. In a nation of Caucasian worshipers, whatever a white person pronounced was a gospel. On the extreme opposite of the racial spectrum, whatever an Asian *gaijin* preached was a nuisance and heretical. Mr. Arai had never heard of an Apple Macintosh computer or MS Word, and because I was the one, and not Anne Neumann, not Jean-Christian or Carolyn Lattin who sought after this new equipment, he was absolutely convinced that it was a "toy," and not a powerful office machine. His argument against buying an Apple Macintosh computer that I heard throughout the first eight months was that if I quit the company - and he was certain that eventually I would - no one else would be able to use this toy. This subtle neglect based on passive racism would not amount to much just this once or twice, but over a year, these little trickles formed a devastating *tsunami,* against which I had absolutely no defense. If I had been a white Caucasian male, I have not probably had to experience this *tsunami* of passive racism. What the managers at the Shiseido Omori International HQ failed to acknowledge was that there was a cumulative effect when a person experiences mounting feelings of injustice at work.[9]

Opportunities tend to seek out wherever there was a vacuum and kinetic discrepancy, and Oscar Godoy was about to fill this vacuum with his two decades of serpentine Japanese experience through the conduit of my Japanese inexperience. By late August of 1993, it became obvious that there was no computer lab, and I had to buy my own Apple Macintosh computer and bring it to the Shiseido Omori International HQ. But how? I knew no used computer stores in Japan. I only knew of the Nippacho, Yokohama, Shinbashi and Omori train stations. So I asked around at the Shiseido Nippacho *Mes Amis* dormitory, and the words got around fast. Soon a dormitory resident that worked at the Shiseido Nippacho Research Laboratory Center approached me during diner one night at the dormitory cafeteria. He was one of the older residents, a Ph.D., who did his honest best to do a good deed by finding me what I needed at the time. Apparently, Apple Macintosh computers were already in wide use by the researchers at the Shiseido Nippacho Research Laboratory Center by 1993. Dr. Takahiko Suwa informed me that there was a man by the name of Oscar Godoy, who taught English at the Shiseido Nippacho Research Laboratory Center once a week, had a used Macintosh for sale, and he was only asking $850. Dr. Suwa showed me the roughly designed flyer. At the bottom of the flyer was the name of the seller, his fax and phone numbers, but no address:

---

[9] - Fortado, Bruce. "The Accumulation of Grievance Conflict." *Journal of Management Inquiry 1.* December (1992): p. 288.

Oscar Godoy
Tel: 0467-47-3266
Fax: 0467-47-0810

Dr. Suwa suggested that I meet with Oscar Godoy. So I did one evening after his English class. He was eager to sell me his used Apple Macintosh Classic II for $850. So eager in fact, he made me nervous. On the same night, he even moved the computer up to my room on the third floor by himself. I wanted to make sure that I was not buying a defective or broken computer, so I asked Oscar to sign a detailed guarantee statement, which I had prepared beforehand. Upon reading it, he proclaimed that he could not sign such an extensive warranty statement, and instead, he hand-wrote the following sentence:

*I, Oscar Godoy, take a full responsibility of one
Apple Macintosh Classic II, 1.4 MB memory and its
accessories for the next 90 days.*

With this guarantee in my hand, I handed Oscar $850 in cash in his Volvo. At the time, I have never imagined that this hand-written document would eventually become the focal point of a 13-month long dispute, symbolizing the essence of what was fundamentally wrong with the Japanese society. Within a month, the reason for Oscar's eagerness to get rid of his Macintosh became clear. I should have test-driven the computer extensively and inquired into the workings of the machine with the latest software before I handed Oscar $850. By early 1993, MS Word 5.0 was available, and it required 2 MB to operate comfortably. Two Microsoft products that were needed the most at the Shiseido Omori International HQ at the time were MS Word and Excel. Between them, they required at least 4 MB to run smoothly. By 1993, 1.4 MB Macintoshes were completely obsolete and useless to run any new software. Back in 1993, memory size was everything for computers, and I made a crucial mistake of not double checking this carefully with Oscar. Oscar was fully aware of this, of course, and this was fueling his heightened eagerness to complete the unfair transaction.

I brought the Apple Macintosh computer to the Shiseido Omori International HQ in the early September through a parcel service, and by the end of September, it was sitting in a box near one of the entrances at the office. It was a sale in which the buyer was obviously misled, and my struggle to get my $850 back from Oscar began. In all honesty, I did not think it would cause such a havoc at the beginning. After all, I had a 90-day hand-written warranty from Oscar, and it could simply be returned to him to get my money back. This assumption was wrong on three major accounts. First, no one at the Shiseido Nippacho Research Laboratory Center or at the Shiseido HR Department knew Oscar's home address. This meant that I would not know exactly where and how to ship the Macintosh back to Oscar. Over two decades of residence in Japan taught Oscar not to list his home address in the telephone directory. For the next three months, I have sent Oscar no less than a dozen faxes, asking for his exact address and refund. He sent me back a letter without a return address and stated in no uncertain terms that because of my "attitude" and "arrogance," he unequivocally refused to return my $850 for the disputed Macintosh computer.

In the early November of 1993, working over 12 hours at a small desktop publishing store in Shibuya, I produced an impressive and comprehensive color presentation set for the annual European marketing conference in Germany. This was the convincing turning point where the practicality of Macintosh computer was finally proven to Messrs. Nagai, Takahashi and Arai. Meanwhile, by the 1993 Christmas holiday time, I was determined to file a small claims suit against Oscar Godoy. I remembered, however, from the first week when I had received a training at the Japan Productivity Center in Shibuya that Japan was a non-litigious society, in which disputes were settled informally outside the judicial system. In collectivist culture, people would rather negotiate than go to court.[10] Since I was in Rome, I had to do as Romans did. Since Mr. Takahashi has been most receptive to my proposal of buying a new Macintosh computer, I recounted my dealings with Oscar Godoy and the stalemate that I was in with Oscar Godoy to Mr. Takahashi. Mr. Takahashi urged me not to file a small claims suit and promised me that he would take care of the problem. I had a strong faith in Mr. Takahashi then, and I had no reason not to believe that he would do otherwise. I was dead wrong - again.

My second false assumption was that Mr. Takahashi would somehow intervene and mitigate the dispute between Oscar and me. In this old and unsophisticated society, when there was a dispute between two parties, the merits of the dispute themselves were rarely questioned. Rather, what is weighted were the social status and positions of the disputants; that is to say, the Japanese social pecking order based on race, gender, age, family name and connections. Thus in Japan, like many places in the world, English-speaking, older, white, Caucasian males comprised the most privileged Brahman caste, immune and shielded from ordinary civil litigation and

---

[10] - Leung, Kwok. "Some determinants of conflict avoidance." *Journal of Cross-Cultural Psychology* 19.1 (1988): pp. 125-136.

exempted from government persecutions. It was precisely in this non-litigious society in which Oscar Godoy has come to master the skills of his trade: Secrecy and legal game of brinkmanship. I could not imagine how many disputes he had dodged and how many thousands of dollars he must have embezzled by simply hiding his home address, and screaming and yelling at anyone who questioned his unscrupulousness. In Britain or the U. S., he would have been sued to death. In Japan, however, his race and gender got him a long, long mileage. Mr. Takahashi could not bear the thought of having to confront a Caucasian male on behalf of an unruly Asian-American employee who has just joined the company, especially considering the fact that Oscar Godoy was a close personal friend of Dr. Ozawa, the highest ranking company official at the Shiseido Nippacho Research Laboratory Center. Mr. Takahashi's strategy, therefore, was to buy up some time by giving me false promises until the whole incident would somehow fade away from my memory and I would give up completely on the case. Oscar Godoy was fully aware of these inner workings of the Japanese system and was ready to play the game of brinkmanship to the full tilt. He was ready to go to full Monty, and so was I.

With the major contribution from Olivier Japiot, a French intern from *L'École Nationale d'Administration,* I again produced and delivered a beautiful, color set of corporate presentation materials, using Adobe Illustrator and Photoshop in December of 1993. By the Christmas time, it became utterly clear that the Shiseido Omori International HQ needed to catch up with the rest of the world in office innovation and needed a new Apple Macintosh computer. Ironically enough, though, the first person ever to bring a functional Apple Macintosh computer and a printer was someone else altogether in the Marketing Department. One morning in February of 1994, I was stunned to discover an Apple Macintosh computer sitting on someone's desk in the Marketing Department section. A fairly good resolution printer was hidden beneath the desk to save space. They were all connected and ready to be operated. I was promptly told that the machines belonged to a new transfer to the Marketing Department. His arrival brought an enormous relief to my daily work load. When Oscar Godoy's Macintosh computer failed in September of 1993, I either had to go to the small computer shop in Shibuya or to another department upstairs where there were an Apple Macintosh computer and a printer to do my daily work. Some in my department accused me of not being faithful to work place etiquette by being away from my desk so frequently or even hiding. This brought tons of wrath from many, especially from Mr. Arai.

If only Oscar Godoy had promptly refunded my $850 for the useless Macintosh computer, I would have bought a new Apple Macintosh and a printer with additional $500 or so and brought them to the office. The root cause of my frequent absences from my desk was Oscar Godoy's conniving, artful and evil chicanery, but Mr. Arai could not possibly see beyond the surface, and I was conveniently blamed. Soon after I had discovered the new Macintosh computer in the office, I began to overburden and annoy the new employee in the Marketing Department by constantly using his Macintosh computer. Someone must have complained about this, or Mr. Nagai or Mr. Takahashi must have taken notice of this and was embarrassed. Soon two employees from the Operations Department took me to an Apple Macintosh dealer in Akihabara to check out a few new computers. A magnetic optical drive, an HP bubbler color printer, a scanner, a digital camera and an Apple Macintosh computer with 4 MB memory were shortly thereafter brought to Shiseido International HQ. The new Macintosh computer was equipped with Adobe Illustrator, Photoshop, MS Word, Excel, Persuasion and other softwares. The artists from the Advertising Department, Carolyn Lattin and Jean-Christian began to use the machines immediately. Meanwhile, the Marketing Department has independently also purchased an Apple Macintosh Duo Power Book laptop computer. Now there were suddenly three Apple Macintosh computers at the Shiseido Omori International HQ, and a new era of window-based, desktop publishing and computing office innovation has finally begun. At last, the Shiseido Omori International HQ caught up with the rest of the computing world. This was exactly eight months after I had joined Shiseido. I was extremely pleased to have a computer of my own at last, and my productivity skyrocketed. I was rejoiced. Everyone ought to be rejoiced, too, but the reality worked exactly the opposite because this new development further exposed the backwardness, computing ignorance and inertia - in a nutshell, what was fundamentally wrong with the company - out in the open, and this was executed not by a white *gaijin* employee, which would have been somewhat tolerable, but by a *gaijin* Asian employee. This enraged many people at the office. None more so than Mr. Arai, and there still was the issue of Oscar Godoy, from whom I had to have my $850 back. The window-based computing era had an uneasy start at the Shiseido Omori International HQ, but there were presentations to be made, faxes to be written and new markets to be opened in Finland, Turkey, Israel and duty-free. The business had to go on.

In Bristol, Birmingham or Bogotá, Oscar Godoy would have been a low-down street hustler, but because this was Yokohama, Oscar was a *bona fide* "English" teacher in a classroom, instead. His race was his diploma and his English accents were his qualifications. While the Macintosh computer upheaval went on at the Omori office, Oscar steadfastly ignored the onslaught of my faxes and hand-delivered letters through my dormitory mates, asking for the return of $850 for the obsolete Macintosh. As far as he was concerned, the transaction between him and me was final and complete. What could possibly go wrong? He must have thought. He was a personal friend of the biggest fish at the Shiseido Nippacho Research Laboratory Center, and he was a Caucasian. Never mind the 90-day warranty. Over at the Shiseido Omori International HQ, I too was steadfast in pressing on about the issue of the refund. I wanted my money back, and it had to come directly from Oscar Godoy himself. I would accept no other settlement.

Because I understood exactly what was fueling Oscar's bizarre behavior, I no longer perceived the dispute as a money issue, but as a racial issue. This type of shenanigan based on race and gender must be stopped. Except while he was away on a seminar to India and Maine, I begged Mr. Takahashi at least once in every fortnight to get in touch with Dr. Ozawa and expose the bully tactics that Oscar Godoy was pulling on me. I did so assiduously from January to July of 1994. This dark cloud of Oscar Godoy scandal was constantly hovering over my every minute of conscious existence in Japan. Just as was the cause with my tenacity to bringing a Macintosh computer to the office, my unrelenting pursuit with the Oscar Godoy scandal further angered a lot of people at the Omori office. My tenacity exposed the backwardness, collective impotence, racial inequality and inertia dealing with Caucasian *gaijin* employees at the Shiseido. It reaffirmed the fact that there indeed was a double standard and a preferential treatment policy toward white *gaijin* employees. This angered many people at the office. None more so than Mr. Arai.

By the first anniversary date of the Macintosh purchase from Oscar Godoy, I was ready to file a small claims suit against him, but before I filed the suit, I wanted to obey the Japanese non-litigious custom and talk to Oscar one last time in person. This was no ordinary task, however. Omori to Nippacho, where the Shiseido Nippacho Research Laboratory Center was located, was exactly an hour away by train. Oscar's English class ended at 6 o'clock, so it meant that I had to break away from my work at the Omori office by 4:45 PM in order to catch Oscar before his class was over, or he would quickly drove away to Kamakura in his new Volvo sedan.

So Oscar Godoy and I met once again for the first time in nearly a year at the Shiseido Nippacho Research Laboratory Center cafeteria on a typically hot and humid August night. By then I no longer was a naïve American expatriate that I once had been a year ago. I wanted to show him his hand-written guarantee, one last time to catch a sense of how he would justify his obvious misdeeds for the past year. The first meeting did not last long. We exchanged sarcastic greetings and pretentious pleasantries. He said he was in a hurry and promised to talk to me in length on the following week. Now the stage was set for a racial showdown. I went back to his English class again on the following week. He was reading an article from *TIME* on the Tibet/China issue. He was calm and composed in front of his Ph.D. students. When the class was dismissed, he and I sat across a coffee table face-to-face on large sofas. Then it was not long before he lost his cool, and he began to scream and yell at me with profanities. He drove home one specific point, which proved and justified my tenacity:

> "Of all the years I've spent dealing with the
> Filipinos, Chinese and Koreans in Japan, I've
> never come across a low life fucker like you!"

I never lost my cool, and quietly listened, directly looking into his eyes. Only snappy replies I ever gave were, "my sentiments exactly," whenever he unwittingly described the events and my alleged misdeeds that were in essence direct results of his not returning my $850 promptly a year go. For example, he showed me an ad from a local Macintosh magazine that showed how much the Macintosh computer that he had sold me a year ago has now depreciated, which was non-sense, for if he had only refunded $850 promptly a year ago, such depreciation would be no concern of his. I calmly made my positions clear. If he would not return my money soon, I was ready to file a small claims suit. In return, he made his positions clear: If I ever pursued this case any further or file a small claims suit, it would be a "war" between us. On the short walk back down the hill to the Shiseido Nippacho *Mes Amis* dormitory, I could not but stop wondering about his choice of the word, "war" and his intended meaning for it. Oscar would start a war with what army? War? World War II. Atomic bombs. Hiroshima and Nagasaki. That was what Oscar probably meant to remind me. What an ignorant charlatan he was! It was a pure miracle, only possible in Japan that a hard-core racist like Oscar Godoy could become an "English" teacher. Only in Japan. During that short walk back, my dislike of Japan began to intensify. Strange twists in the history of humankind produced this mutant society, people and a bizarre character like Oscar Godoy in this island nation. Oscar must have gotten away from many sticky situations like this by screaming and yelling loudly in English in the past two decades, just as he was trying to do with me just now.

I had suspected from the beginning that the only reason why Oscar Godoy was able to get away with such a conniving criminal behavior was precisely due to the unsophisticated, unjust, racially stratified social structure in Japan, and he had just proved it by referring to my "nationality" in the confrontation. His dismissive obscenity has just proven my suspicion. My deep suspicion has finally been confirmed. That was exactly why I was so adamant about the case, and I was absolutely determined to take Oscar Godoy to a small claim court in Japan. I wanted to expose his and Japan's perverted racially-defined social structure whereby a white *gaijin* person was always right whatever evil he or she committed. The only reason why Oscar Godoy was able to prosper and flourish in Japan was that he happened to be a Caucasian *gaijin* male. He would not be able to function outside Asia, because everyone would sue him to death for his criminal behavior. White was always right in Japan, and he was white in Japan. I would suppose this could be also true in Hong Kong, Korea, Taiwan, the Philippines, Singapore, Thailand, *etc.*

Small Claims Suit against Oscar Godoy
My first strategy was to establish the proper jurisdiction, so I visited district courts in Yokohama, were the transaction between Oscar and me had taken place, and in Kamakura, where the defendant resided. Since it has been over a year, I was also worried about the statute of limitation. I took days off from work and visited the clerks of the districts courts. Eventually, I was led to a volunteer lawyer at the Yokohama Civic Center near the Yokohama Station who coached me on the intricacies of the Japanese legal system and litigation. Soon I learned that the proper jurisdiction of my case was in Yokohama; that all documents had to be translated into Japanese; and that the plaintiff must list on the complaint writ the home address of the defendant. So my search for Oscar's home address began. I went to the Japanese DMV with Oscar's Volvo license plate number for the public registration document. His car was registered in his brother's name. I visited Kamakura several times, explaining to the police officers and civil servants at the foreign national registry of my plight, begging for the disclosure of Oscar's home address. Those foolish civil servants thought that protecting personal information of a Caucasian *gaijin* man was a national and civic duty, short of an indisputable evidence of a murder, and they would not disclose Oscar's home address in Kamakura. What a utterly pathetic country Japan was! When I communicated my inability to find out Oscar's home address at the next appointment, the kind volunteer lawyer suggested that I use the work address of Oscar Godoy; *i. e.,* Shiseido Nippacho Research Laboratory Center

on the complaint document instead, but this would mention and implicate Shiseido's name on a civil litigation and would further enrage Mr. Arai. This would mean finally that I had to quit the company because I would be naming my employer, Shiseido, as the defendant and biting the hand that was feeding me. But in this game of legal brinkmanship that Oscar was playing with me, that was what the whole case boiled down to: *Pierce Parker versus Oscar Godoy and Shiseido Nippacho Research Laboratory Center.*

Just as well. By late September of 1994, I was absolutely sick of the predicament which I was forced into, and I wanted to return to California, no matter how disgraceful and disappointing it might be. I wrote a letter of resignation to the Shiseido HR Department and gave a 30-day notice, as mandated by the renewed employment contract, which I had just signed only a few weeks ago. Because of the light case load at the small claims court in Yokohama, the trial date was set for mid-November of 1994. I was not going to attend the trial. I thought I lost the case. No matter what I did in Japan and no matter how brilliant I was in Japan, I would always loose because of my race. I thought that was exactly what I was trying to escape from when I had left the U. S. for Japan in July of 1993. I was too quixotic, searching for that illusive Promised Land with social justice: *Liberté, egalité, fraternité.* But the experience that I have had in Japan during the past year did not live up to my expectations. I was to return to the U. S. in the first week of November, 1994. I received an approval for holidays, which I had never used during my entire stay, from Mr. Takahashi for the last two weeks of October, 1994, and I re-visited the places that I have frequented for one last time in Shibuya, Shinji-ku, Yokohama, Roppongi and Ginza. During this period, Mr. Kanda harassed me as if the world was coming to an end soon. To him, I was a free loader who never went to the office for the two weeks, and he could not wait to get rid of me from his dormitory. He degraded and belittled me at every chance he could get and for every excuse he could think of. Only two days after I actually had filed the small claims law suit against Oscar Godoy, using his Shiseido work address, Mr. Takahashi had a copy of the complaint given to him from the corporate lawyer at the Shiseido Omori International HQ. I did not know exactly how the corporate lawyer had gotten hold of the copy, but I suspected that he was notified from the Shiseido Nippacho Research Laboratory Center. I felt that I had a moral obligation to inform Dr. Suwa that I was going to file a lawsuit against Oscar Godoy, justify my action and seek a blessing by giving Dr. Suwa a copy of the complaint in advance. It must have been that Dr. Suwa notified someone at the Shiseido Nippacho Research Laboratory Center, and then the corporate lawyer at the Shiseido Omori International HQ was notified. Another possibility was that the clerk at the Yokohama District Court phoned and faxed a copy of my complaint document to the Shiseido Nippacho Research Laboratory Center.

In either way, I was summoned to a small meeting by Messrs. Arai and Takahashi at a conference room a few days after the law suit was filled. Mr. Arai by then was newly appointed as the vice president of Shiseido France, S. A., and he was only a few days away from being permanently transferred to Paris. He made a forceful point to withdraw the law suit at once. He insisted that such an aggressive behavior by me undermined the "harmony," or *wha,* of the company, as he has been telling me for many months. Incidentally, he has used this breaking "harmony" theory countless times with me every time something occurred. I acknowledge now that in one occasion, he was correct; namely, the time when I neglected to attend the wedding of a staff member in the International Business Department II in order to save ¥30,000 out of my inter-cultural ignorance. Mr. Arai promised that the company would pay me ¥70,000 to settle the case out of court. I, of course, had absolutely no intention of withdrawing my suit. After all, it was no longer a monetary issue, but a racial issue. Nonetheless, I insincerely promised to do exactly as I was instructed by repeating "yes" many times to whatever Mr. Arai said. This was a negotiating tactic that I learned specifically from no other than Mr. Takahashi himself in Japan: Just say "yes" to whatever the other party demanded. I needed not actually perform the demand.

Mr. Takahashi ought to know. He has not been fulfilling his promise for the past six months with my requests to intervene in the Oscar Godoy scandal. The next morning, Mr. Takahashi rushed toward me after speaking frenetically with someone on the phone and brandishing ¥10,000 bills in his hand. He had ¥70,000 in his hand and wanted to hand it to me. I politely declined his offer and again insincerely promised him that I would withdraw the lawsuit against Oscar Godoy immediately. I had absolutely no such intention. It was time now to gently let Mr. Takahashi taste his own medicine. Little did they know that by engaging in such collectivist behaviors, Messrs. Arai and Takahashi were passively supporting - in fact implicitly encouraging - continued survival and existence of an evil shenanigan character like Oscar Goody in Japan.

For sometime now, Dr. Tatsuya Ozawa must have known about the dispute between Oscar Godoy and me, too. I was briefly introduced to Dr. Ozawa at a summer festival at the Shiseido Nippacho Research Laboratory Center back in August of 1993, only several days after my arrival in Japan. Several times after the initial introduction, he and I came face-to-face at various venues. My name must not have registered in his mind prominently until the Oscar Godoy scandal broke out in the spring of 1994. I had been under a strict order from Mr. Takahashi not to contact Dr. Ozawa directly about the Oscar Godoy case. I was told that such a direct contact was improper and was unacceptable in the Japanese social protocol. So I refrained myself from visiting his house, phoning or faxing him. On one afternoon in August of 1994 at the Shiseido Omori International HQ, however, I ran into him once again in the elevator. Apparently, he was at the Shiseido Omori International HQ to attend a division-wide meeting, and I stopped him. Although I did not present him my interpretation on the root of the case - racism - I did spill out my guts and explained passionately the conniving swindle that Oscar Godoy was pulling on me. Dr. Ozawa must have been puzzled by my passionate lecture. This was Japan. This was simply not done, especially by a non-Caucasian *gaijin*. He quietly listened for ten minutes or so and was quickly led away to the meeting by his assistants. In Japan, the highest badge of social honor and prestige was to have a personal Caucasian *gaijin* friend. It meant that one was very hip, educated, civilized, polished and an honorary white person. It did not matter whether the white *gaijin* friend was from Estonia, Kazakhstan, Columbia or Turkmenistan, as long as the friend was racially Caucasian, it worked. In Japan, white was always right. To challenge the genuineness and integrity of Dr. Ozawa's emblem of social prestige, especially by a non-Caucasian *gaijin*, was a fantastic blasphemy. Thus, my behavior puzzled Dr. Ozawa beyond any description.

Unbeknownst to me, in the mean time, the machinery of the Oscar Godoy scandal was making a dramatic Shakespearean turn. On the Saturday before my departure back to the U. S., I went back to the Shiseido Omori International HQ one last time to collect my personal belongings I might have forgotten. To my shock, I found a fax from Oscar Godoy on the fax machine. Oscar Godoy finally conceded to give me back my $850 upon my return of the disputed Macintosh to the security office at the Shiseido Nippacho Research Laboratory Center! I was still highly incredulous, and I saw it as yet another one of Oscar Godoy's long series of unscrupulous time-buying tactics. It turned out to be sincere, however. A fellow Ph.D. dorm resident, who was a student of Oscar Godoy, acted as a go-between, and as soon as I returned two boxes filled with the Macintosh and the accessories to the security office at the Shiseido Nippacho Research Laboratory Center, Oscar Godoy wired back $850 to my bank account on October 26, 1994. This was less than a week before my departure back to the U. S. and exactly 14 months after the original purchasing date. This long and excruciating saga has finally come to a just end.

Seizing the opportunity, meanwhile, Mr. Kanda was furious on me once again for bringing down and keeping my "personal belongings" in the mail room before I brought them to the security office at the Shiseido Nippacho Research Laboratory Center. These "personal belongings" contained the disputed Macintosh computer, the symbol of Shiseido's backwardness and my own remedy to it, but to Mr. Kanda, those boxes proved again that I was nothing but a trouble-making "Korean" who had no respect for his authority. He scolded and yelled at me as usual; by now, he has done it so frequently that it lost any meaning, but was an irrelevant noise to me. Just as well. To his low intelligence and pitiful level of education, Mr. Kanda would never figure out the true significance and meaning of those boxes and the noble attempts that I had made for my company, his company, and Oscar Godoy's company, Shiseido. Ignorance was truly bliss.

On July 12, 1998 in Paris, five years after these events had taken place, Jean-Christian de La Chevalerie had a critical final analysis on the outcome of the Oscar Godoy fiasco. He outlined three possible scenarios. The first version, the one that I wished was true, was that Oscar was gravely scared by my tenacity and by the small claims lawsuit. He was truly frightened by the prospect of being humiliated at the small claims court. In other words, I had finally "won" the peculiar game of brinkmanship against Oscar Godoy. On the other hand, however, knowing Japan as well as Jean-Christian did and having worked together with me at the Shiseido over a year, this version seemed too incongruous to him.

The second possibility he formulated was that someone, perhaps a high-ranking officer at the Shiseido HR Department, or Dr. Ozawa himself, specifically ordered Oscar Godoy to return $850 back to me, after weighing the merits of the dispute, with a threat of dismissal.

The third likely scenario was that someone from the Shiseido Omori International HQ, possibly Mr. Takahashi or Mr. Nagai, gave the $850 to Oscar Godoy and begged him to end the dispute by wiring it to my bank account so that it would appear as if $850 came directly from Oscar Godoy. Stated differently, someone wanted to make me think that I "won" the dispute. Any one of these scenarios could well have been true. Yet there was a powerful lesson to be learned from this ordeal. White supremacy and its hegemonic effects were a universal phenomenon, and not confined to just the U. S. or France. They were and are everywhere on this planet.

The exact home address of Oscar Godoy in Kamakura is still to this date unknown.

CHAPTER 6

White Women in Japan

White women occupy a strange position in Japanese society.
According to the Japanese sexist doctrine, they ought to be hierarchically
below Japanese men, but they are white, so how do the Japanese reconcile
this dilemma? The answer is that the race trumps the gender. White women
may be female, but they are nevertheless white. A white woman in Japan,
therefore, enjoys a full privileged status as a white person, rather than
subordinated status as a woman. The radio talk show host, Rush Limbaugh,
once declared sometime ago that the women's rights movement in the U. S.
existed just so that unattractive women could gain access to the mainstream.
Likewise, using his lingo, it could be said that Japan existed just so that
unattractive white women could gain instant access to its mainstream. So the
second-rate American models would become supermodels in Japan, and
outback countrywomen from Australia would flourish instantly in the
Japanese print and advertisement industries. So long as they were white, they
were fair dunkum. It is often said stereotypically that Japanese men mistreat
women. This is incorrect. Japanese men mistreat Asian, black and Latino
women. They never mistreat Caucasian women. Japanese men have a keen
awareness of their whiteness.

While I was in Japan, I was becoming sick and tired of being belittled
by Australians, Israelis, and New Zealanders at Roppongi as to "why I spoke
English so well." Those young people that came to Japan to work in 1993
and 1994 came with mentalities that they simply planned to make a short stay
there to make quick bucks - no more, no less. They were fair-weather friends
to Japan so long as the yen remained strong. I felt, therefore, that they had
absolutely no respect for the Japanese people, culture, language, or customs.
I sensed further that they operated on a racial superiority complex for their
being Caucasians in an Asian country. The Australian, American, Canadian,

Israeli and New Zealander women that I have met in Japan probably never perceived me as a human being, but as a highly-racialized Asian object who happened "to speak English so well." They, therefore, interacted with me strikingly differently from how they would normally interact with a white male in that their aim was to exploit and to squeeze out as much money and booty out of me as possible, rather than seeking a healthy, normal relationship. This became very obvious about six months into my stay in Japan. In such highly-racially objectified context, I could never have operated with a sound mind, and it took a heavy toll in my psychological well-being. Due to the mostly negative experiences that I have had with the white women described below in Japan, I felt as if I received all the discrimination that a *gaijin* would normally receive in Japan, but I never was a recipient of any privilege that a white *gaijin* was entitled to in Japan, both from the Japanese *and* the Caucasians. By September of 1994, therefore, I wished to leave Japan as soon as possible. Remembering that I had gone to a better life, not a miserable life, I knew I had to leave.

Broadly speaking, the white women that I encountered in Japan could be categorized into four distinct classes. The first class was comprised of corporate professionals. They were working as career women in large Japanese multinationals. They chose to come to Japan due to the favorable exchange rate of the Yen at the time. They were highly educated individuals with advanced degrees and a high level of Japanese language proficiency. The second class was made up of those that worked as English teachers. These were often recent college graduates who ventured out to Japan to experience a different culture and life-style. The third class was made up of those that just happened to wander into Japan while they were backpacking around the world through various avenues and channels for temporary employment reasons. These included jewelry sellers on the streets by the train stations and the bar hostesses that worked at various spots in Roppongi. The most intriguing and mysterious class, however, was the fourth class of Caucasian women who came to Japan specifically to work in the local sex industry of various types. They included women from Australia, Brazil, Canada, Columbia, Russia and the U. S. I regret tremendously now that I failed to investigate more extensively as to how they managed to make the contacts for their employment in Tokyo. To the women that belong to this class, Japan was their Wild West. There were no kindergarten class mates, relatives, teachers or clergy to recognize their faces and regulated their sexual activities in Japan, so their sexual liberty was guaranteed. Described below are the white women that I encountered in Japan. Because Tokyo was a small town as far as the spheres of activities were concerned for these women, I often ran into them on the streets and train stations again and again. I have distinct memories of all of them. I wonder where they are now.

Anne Neumann

I had read about Anne Neumann in a DISCO Company magazine article before I actually met her for the first time along with Jean-Christian de La Chevalerie and Cameron Brown in Shibuya in July of 1993. Cameron Brown and Anne Neumann sitting next to each other reminded me of Lloyd Bensen and Dan Qualye standing next to each other at a 1992 Vice Presidential debate. One was obviously a lot more mature and seasoned than the other was. Anne Neumann was prominently featured in the article as the first white American young woman working for a major Japanese cosmetics company. She was in charge of newly opened Portuguese, Danish and Swedish markets in the European Section of the International Business Department II. She had lived in Japan before in her high school years as a Rotarian exchange student. She was a Monica Lewinsky look-alike who wore bright red lipsticks and impeccable make-up everyday to the office. She was a spectacularly ordinary person who had a perpetual immunity and whose mistakes and misdeeds were always forgiven for the virtue of her race and gender in Japan. She was a graduate of the University of Michigan at Ann Arbor and had spent sometime also in Italy before coming to Japan. She was neither a genius, nor an idiot. She was plainly decent and ordinary person who executed her given duties well and by the book. In Kalamazoo, she would have been an administrative assistant at a used car dealership or an auto part plant, but in Japan, her ordinary whiteness has catapulted her into the stratosphere of fame, glory, prestige and privilege. At Shiseido, she represented everything that was going well with the company, and she was receiving a goddess-like celebrity treatment.

I once saw a picture of her at the signing ceremony with the new Swedish distributor. This must have been just a few months after she had been hired in 1992. She was decked up like a department store cosmetics counter sales woman with an immaculate make-up, bright red lipsticks and greased pulled-back hair. She was exactly like the women from Robert Palmer's *Addicted to Love* music video. She was seated conspicuously at the head of the table right next to Messrs. Nagai and Arai, directly facing the Swedish delegates. Mr. Miyazaki, the Japanese employee who must have done the most of the ground work, was seated at the corner in the background. Anne Neumann seemed to be enjoying her new role as the living poster child for Shiseido. By the time I met her in July of 1993, she was no longer doing so, but in the picture she was proudly wearing a Shiseido company lapel pin. Anne Neumann came to work everyday with an impeccable makeup. She kept this up until she left Shiseido. One might psychoanalyze that she was under a heavy pressure to maintain her image up while she was at Shiseido, whatever that "image" might have been.

My relationship with Anne Neumann went through several stages until I came to resent her tremendously for her privileges. There was nothing fundamentally wrong with her personality or character, but I am fairly certain now that she felt my resentment. Looking back, for she was merely an actress who had to play the role given to her based on the scripts at a theater that was Japan, my resentment should have been directed against the script writers, the directors and the production company, but not at her. She was merely an actress playing her part. I owe her my deep and sincere apology in that sense. So Anne Neumann character that I came to resent could have been any young white Caucasian woman at the Shiseido Omori International HQ. I used to call Anne Neumann pejoratively a "Queen Bee" or "Q. B.," because the alpha female character she was groomed to play in her full glory was best described by that epithet. It was not beyond the realm of imagination that in a sea of middle-aged Japanese salary worker bees, she commanded somewhat of a privileged authority, as though she had a privy to a body of knowledge no other employee at the Shiseido Omori International HQ had by sheer force of her race.

In her mid-twenties, she was already an honorary general executive director at the Shiseido Omori International HQ. It was a sight to be hold and to see when she gave directions and orders to middle-aged managers. In Japan, sexism is just as strong as racism. Female employees were expected to perform such menial duties as serving teas and making photocopies, but because she was a Caucasian female employee, she was specifically exempted from the traditional Japanese gender role. Not that I concurred with such sexist gender roles, but that I could not accept the exemption she was deliberately given *because* of her race. I have not once seen her serving tea to anyone. For the first three months, our relationship was very cordial and polite, then my sense of resentment began to develop. By 1993, it was her second year of employment with Shiseido, and as outlined in her employment contract, she was awarded a free round-trip ticket to and from her hometown in Michigan for the Christmas. There was nothing unusual about this Christmas trip home, except that she was also given a grand tour of New York City in a sweet-heart deal as a part of the Christmas holiday package. I learned about this only a few days before her actual departure in December of 1993. There was a direct flight into Chicago or Detroit from Tokyo via Northwest Airlines, and her detour to New York City was extremely unusual, to say the least. The official reason for this free grand tour of New York City was to let Anne Neumann get acquainted with the staff members of Shiseido Cosmetics America, Inc. in Manhattan, but I knew better that the true reason was to give her some special incentive so that she would stay with the company because she was a white Caucasian woman. (See the draft of the fax addressed to Shisiedo Cosmetics America, which was never sent at Jean-Christian's refrain in Appendices.)

From the time she returned from the Christmas break in January of 1994 until the day I left Japan in November of 1994, I rarely spoke to her unless it was absolutely necessary. My resentment against her solidified like a hot burning stove over the Christmas and New Year's break in 1993. I was constantly degraded and belittled by Mr. Kanda at the Shiseido Nippacho *Mes Amis* dormitory in a far away remote place called Nippa in Kanagawa Prefecture. I was lonely in a strange land without any friends, entertainment, a TV, a telephone or a car. Whereas Anne Neumann was given a laptop computer of her own from the company, I have not had a computer of my own yet, which made my workload painfully tedious and difficult. Moreover, she was living at an apartment in Omori only a few minutes from the office, and her apartment was paid by the company. Furthermore, Oscar Godoy was defrauding me $850 and steadfastly refusing to return my money. People evaluate their resources by comparing them to resources of other people and to what they have experience in the past.[11] One could reasonably predict that this relative deprivation was linked to my feelings of anger and resentment.[12] Thus, I began to reason that if I too had been a white employee, I needed not experience the same misery and have the same pitiful predicament that I was forced into. In my close psychological and physical proximity to Anne Neumann, I rightfully concluded that if I too had been a white employee, Shiseido would have been more eager to look after my welfare in Japan. I wanted to know why she was able to live at a private apartment paid by Shiseido near the office in Omori while I had to commute two hours everyday in hyper-crowded trains from Yokohama to Omori. I questioned why she was able to go out to Roppongi on weekends and was still able to return to her apartment by a taxi in Omori, whereas I had to spend over $200 to take a taxi back to Nippacho in Kanagawa Prefecture or had to check into a capsule hotel for $80. I inquired why she was able to bring anyone she liked back to her

---

[11] - Runciman, Walter Garrison. *Relative deprivation and social justice.* Berkeley: University of California Press, 1966.

[12] - Crosby, Faye. "A model of egoistical relative deprivation." *Psychological review* 83.2 (1976): p. 85; Crosby, Faye. "Relative Deprivation in Organizational Settings." *Research in Organizational Behavior,* 6 (1984): pp. 51–93; and *Ibid.,* Runciman.

apartment and have love fests, whereas I was not allowed to bring anyone back to the Shiseido Nippacho *Mes Amis* dormitory. I asked myself why she has had a personal laptop computer for her own use, when I had to wait for a Macintosh computer for nearly nine months at Shiseido. I inquired why she was given a free trip to New York City from Shiseido during the 1993 Christmas break. There were simply too many questions that I raised which could only be answered by the racial factor. So how did I deal with this feeling of inequity? When people find themselves participating in an inequitable relationship, they become distressed. The greater the perceived inequality, the more distressed people feel.[13] I became extremely disillusioned at the office and began *clowning.* I started to bring donuts to the office and distributed them. I began to dress up like a Mafia man by wearing Versace silk shirts to the office. I made and served Hazelnut-flavored coffee sent from the U. S., as if to drive a point as to how ridiculous it was to require only the female employees to serve tea and coffee, but at the same time to have Anne Neumann exempted from this traditional gender role simply because of her race. I started to repeat the phrase, "You are a good man. God bless you," which I heard from *Schindler's List,* again and again whenever I engaged myself in a conversation at the office. I commenced to spread the gospels of Marx and Lenin to whoever listened. This was to point out the strange capitalistic society that the white supremacy has managed to create in Japan. To counter the hardship of the long commute and the unbearable humidity, I started to carry around a shopping bag with a change of clothes. As soon as I arrived at the Omori office, I went to the men's room first, changed and walked into the office. I carried around this shopping bag wherever I went. Moreover, one typical response of people who experience inequities is to engage more in activities they enjoy than in those that needed to be done,[14] so I began to spend a lot of time perfecting the Shiseido corporate presentation materials.

For the first few months, she probably was glad to have another fellow American expatriate on board in her department, but the jubilation quickly fizzled away. She felt my resentment, and I feverishly resented her for her insensitivity to see this utterly obvious unequal fix, as a fellow American expatriate working so physically and psychologically closely together, that she was given a preferential treatment simply because of her race; for taking advantage of this apparent racial inequality; for not speaking up against it and not refusing forthrightly to accept such special treatment in the interest of equality. In retrospect, however, it was unavoidable. After all, she had not

---

[13] - *Ibid.,* Thompson, p. 197.

[14] - *Ibid.,* Cook, Hunsaker and Coffey, p. 236.

come to Japan on a crusade to champion a civil rights movement. She was simply a spectacularly ordinary white woman who came to Japan to work, and I was spectacularly disappointed at her: Did it not mean that being an American entailed standing up for our national creed that all human beings are created equal? So I resented her, for being a more privileged American than I was in Japan. There was no Equal Employment Opportunity Officer at Shiseido to address my resentments.

There were two memorable events at the Omori office that added fuel to my resentment against Anne Neumann. On February 21, 1994, at the Shiseido Omori International HQ, work was halted by Mr. Arai, and everyone was summoned to the smoking room in the back of the office. Mr. Arai ostentatiously did this in order to celebrate Anne Neumann's 25th or 26th birthday. An elaborate cake was purchased, and everyone was treated with hearty drinks. There was nothing extraordinary about the small birthday celebration - after all, it was done all the time throughout the world - except that it was the *only* birthday work stoppage ever explicitly dictated by Mr. Arai, ever. Needless to say, my birthday in January, or anybody else's for that matter, was neither acknowledged nor noted. In this sense, Anne Neumann was a company pet, and a very privileged one at that.

St. Patrick's Days are very important to me, and I tend to remember events that happen around St. Patrick's Days. On March 17, 1994, I was chewing a gum in the office because I had bad breathe. It was a bad judgment on my part, especially in Japan, where the office work environment was considered more formal and serious. I was oblivious to all this on that particular day because I had seen others in the office chewing gum before, but when Mr. Arai saw me, he summoned me forthwith to the end of the department desk row and accosted me to spit the gum out at once. I complied without any questions. Again, there was nothing unusual about this reprimand, except that on the next day Anne Neumann was flagrantly chewing gum right next to Mr. Arai. At first, I thought it was some type of a practical joke, remembering the aggressiveness displayed by Mr. Arai in correcting my transgression just yesterday, but this time he was saying absolutely nothing, and he was doing his work at his desk as usual. I was amazed and stunned by his hypocritical contraction, but I did not speak up. By that time, I learned the ways of the Japanese racial discrimination. As I was carefully observing Mr. Arai and Anne Neumann silently working shoulder-to-shoulder next to each other, the noise from Anne's chewing the gum echoed loudly in my head. I made a sharp entry on my mental discrimination awareness bank account book. All was well at the Shiseido Omori International HQ, except that my hot stone of resentment was burning more vigorously than ever. Although I have never had any confrontational episode with Anne Neumann, my actions spoke volumes. I avoided her at all cost, for I perceived her not as my compatriot, but as my Caucasian alter ego. One could say that racial tensions at the Omori office were extremely high in those days.

Yet my life in Japan went on, and Anne Neumann was executing her duties well in a spectacularly ordinary way, albeit she has made some mistakes along the way. The Shiseido company norm dictated that she would receive a sweetheart treatment and more extrinsic rewards because she was a white Caucasian employee. She was once the employee with the highest overtime working hours, despite the company-wide directive to cut down on overtimes. She lived only a few minutes away from the office. She was, therefore, opted to have a lot more overtime hours. I, on the other hand, would have never been able to do the same. After all, I lived an hour away from the Omori office in Kanagawa Prefecture. Equalization of overtime should mean that all employees must have equal opportunity to work overtime,[15] but this never was the case. I felt a strong racial discrimination bias working against me at the Omori office as the managers at the Shiseido Omori International HQ evaluated Anne Neumann's actions on the basis of her racial affiliation, rather than on the merits of her behaviors themselves. My sensing the racial discrimination bias in Japan was not unique. Other non-white workers reported the same experience recently (*Vide* the *San Jose Mercury News* article in Appendices). I strongly suspected that feeling of discrimination was one of the main reasons why an Asian-American female employee before me, Kathy Ho, had decided to quit Shiseido abruptly only a few weeks before my arrival under the pretense of "getting married to her boyfriend" back in the U. S. Apparently, she precipitously left Shiseido only a month after renewing her employment contract for the second year. Unless otherwise she had renewed the employment contract, she would not have received the last month's salary from Shiseido on a technical ground because the last month's salary was paid in the next month, and thus only if she had renewed the employment contract and stayed with Shiseido for another month, she would have received the past month's salary. This was exactly how I had to quit the company, too. The details of my employment contract renewal negotiation are described more extensively below under the *Employment Contract Renewal Negotiation* chapter.

Anne Neumann and I met a few times in Roppongi by chance. She could afford to stay out late on weekends because her apartment was only $20

---

[15] - Morrison, William F. *The Prenegotiation Planning Book.* New York: John Wiley & Sons, Inc. (1985): p. 191.

or so taxi ride away from Roppongi. In fact, she once told me that she rode her bicycle to Roppongi. I would have never been able to do the same. After all, I lived 90 minutes away from Roppongi, and if I should miss the last train at midnight, it meant that I had to either spend $200 for a taxi ride back to Nippacho or $80 for an overnight stay at a capsule hotel somewhere. Thus, Anne Neumann's experience of Japan and mine were as different as night and day.

According to Jean-Christian, Anne Neumann became pregnant and decided to quit Shiseido shortly after I left Japan in November of 1994. She is now married to a Latin American man and works for the Shiseido Latin America office in Miami, Florida. Kerry, one of the original Shiseido Girls, introduced Anne Neumann to her current husband.

Carolyn Lattin

Carolyn Lattin was from Dana Point, California and was another American expatriate, working in the Marketing Department at the Shiseido Omori International HQ. Her father was a doctor in the Southern California. Along with Anne Neumann, she was often given a time-off to serve as a guinea pig for those Shiseido beauty consultants that were about to go abroad to practice applying make-ups, as if she and Anne Neumann were the perfect specimens of white femaleness and on the grounds that the beauty consultants needed Caucasian faces on which to practice their make-up application skills. She was a Mount Holyoke graduate who was appointed as the anchorwoman at the spring new product introduction conference in March of 1994 precisely because she was a white woman. Jean-Christian and I used to call her"Queen Bee II," or "Q. B. II," then deviated to "Quarterback II" after Anne Neumann. My relationship with Carolyn Lattin went through a few stages until I came to resent her very much, just as was the case with Anne Neumann. The following confrontation epitomized my resentment:

It happened on July 15, 1994 around 1:15 PM. She asked me "what my first language was," and she was asking me "whether I knew who Kathy Ho was." I was typing a document with the Macintosh Duo laptop computer right next to Carolyn Lattin. Earlier that morning, I had asked Carolyn Lattin to proofread a recommendation letter requested by Mr. Takahashi on the Macintosh computer screen. In the course of this casual conversation, I imitated the Southern judge in the movie, *My Cousin Vinny,* and I pronounced the "h" in "vehemently."

To this, Carolyn Lattin brusquely barked, "You have a funny accent. What is your first language?" In order to grant her a graceful exit by the way of my deliberate miscomprehension, I replied, "Pierce." Yet she was very unrelenting and shouted, "I meant your first language, not your first name!"

At this point, I resorted to silence in order to allow Carolyn Lattin to realize the true magnitude of what she has just belched, but she continued, "You seemed to be distressed."

So I replied, "You sensed it well." Then a long silence followed, then I broke the ice, "Are you offended that I took an offense?"

She was invincible: "Why are you offended?"

I calmly explained, "What exactly was your connotation?"

She said defensively, "You were making a grammatical mistake that was certainly not from a person with a European first language-based."

By this reply, I was dead certain that her inquiry and motive was solely relied on race. "Oh, yeah, not a European, ha? Where are you basing your judgment?" I quickly replied.

Then this reply waffled out from her mouth, "Just drop it, but like the grammatical mistakes you made on the recommendation letter and the mistakes on the presentation you made with Olivier Japiot!"

I immediately countered, "Is it possible that those mistakes were made by Olivier?"

She countered, "No, because he told me you wrote them, Pierce, just drop it."

Another period of silence ensued as we typed away quietly. She finally accosted, "Are you accusing me of being prejudiced?"

To this, I said, "a passive one."

Then she released odious slights, "How could I be prejudiced when my boyfriends in the past have been Indian and Chinese and other Asians? I am not prejudiced against Asians!"

I have heard this love-prejudice justification from previous condition of existence as the ground for not being prejudiced so many times before, so I replied, "Of course, not. As long as they are subservient, why should you be? Look, it should never occur to me that I should criticize your English because you are white - white is always right, right?" I was going to be more sarcastic by saying, "You are an asianophile, ha? Just like Dana Jourdan, herself." But I refrained myself.

To make the matter worse in the confrontation, Carolyn Lattin brought up Kathy Ho, "Do you remember Kathy Ho? She quit to get married? She spoke just like you."

To this I replied, "What do I have common with her?"

To this, she continued, "She was a Chinese-American girl, remember her?"

I replied, "I must be a Chinese, then. No, I have not met her at all, but I have a theory as to why she had to quit. She quit because she felt discriminated against for being a Chinese-American."

And this was the last sentence I ever spoke to Carolyn Lattin at Shiseido: "If I had been white, what would you say those mistakes were?"

This racial episode with Carolyn Lattin was one of the major reasons that made me decide to quit Shiseido as soon as possible. I saw her action as the perfect representation of the sentiments harbored by the other employees; namely Mr. Arai, Mr. Kanda and Oscar Godoy. Although I apologized to her several weeks later for this episode, I have never forgotten the ill feelings. In retrospect, it was true that she was an asianophile to a certain degree. She seemed to have possessed an unusually highly degree of love-prejudice toward Asian males, as she has declared in the above confrontation, yet at the same time, she seemed to have also possessed a high degree of racial insensitivity and superiority attitude towards them. In retrospect, it was more than possible that she had come to Japan specifically to find a husband. I once accidentally overheard her conversation with Dana Jourdan at the Ginza main office after all the recent *gaijin* recruits were assembled to an end of the year orientation in December of 1993. She was describing to Dana Jourdan how excited she was, for I have parlayed with her earlier that day and how I "appeared" to like her. Only a few weeks before the above incident, she even invited me to her dormitory under the pretense that she wished to discuss the future direction of the company with others. Due to the above exchange, however, did I not only bother not to go to her dormitory, but I never spoke of this proposed "meeting" ever again. In her condescending white supremacy insensitivity, she failed to see that there was not a chance in hell that I could reciprocate her curiosity, given the unequal racial context that we were both placed under. In the spring of 1994, her housing arrangement was upgraded to a better one by the Shiseido HR Department in Heiwajima with the renewal of her employment contract. Because of this, she was now able to commute to the Shiseido Omori International HQ on foot in 15 minutes. Carolyn Lattin had no way of knowing the pathetic misery that I was experiencing at the Shiseido Nippacho *Mes Amis* dormitory and the weekly scolding that I was receiving from Mr. Kanda. When the news of her housing upgrade reached me, I suspected instantly that she was given a preferential treatment in housing because of her race, and I resented her profoundly. How could I never develop a fondness for someone who was taking a full advantage of this racial inequality? How could a prey ever appreciate the predator? Had I met her under a different circumstance in a different *milieu,* perhaps in

Northampton, Massachusetts, our understanding of each other might have been more amicable. But at the theater that she and I were both performing at the time, the complexities of the plot and the iniquitous roles given simply did not allow any happy liaison. It must have been a fate. Carolyn Lattin now works at the American subsidiary of Shiseido in New Jersey.

Dana Jourdan

The very first Caucasian woman that I encountered in Japan was Dana Jourdan. She was a German expatriate who spoke and wrote Japanese and English fluently. I looked up to her, and to this date, my aspiration is to become just like her some day. She was a true international business professional who could operate in all three major global economic blocks. She was assigned in the Shiseido HR Department. She and I had a very unpleasant beginning. On the second day of my arrival in Japan, she was to take me to the Japan Productivity Center in Shibuya, since I was unfamiliar with Tokyo. I had forgotten where exactly at the Yokohama Station she asked me to meet her, so rather than searching for her uselessly in the sea of morning commuters, I simply decided to go ahead and find the Japan Productivity Center in Shibuya on my own. Later, Ms. Ishiwata inquired me as to why I did not telephone into the Shiseido HR Department in Ginza, which could have acted as the information center to find each other. Dana Jourdan did just that. She frantically called the Shiseido HR Department several times that morning to see whether I had called in to report my exact location. The fact of the matter was that I did not know how to work the Japanese pay phone. Unlike the American telephone numbers, there were usually eight digits in a Japanese telephone number, and without having told first, I had no way of knowing whether I had to dial the area code first when I made a call from Yokohama to Tokyo. Nor was there any way for me to know that *all* Japanese pay phones only took telephone cards. So this incident made a very negative first impression of me on her.

I was somewhat intrigued by her superb language proficiencies and apparent engagement to a Japanese man. She was a close ally and a point woman for Carolyn Lattin, and as such, I suspected that she played a major lobbying role in securing an upgraded housing arrangement at the Shiseido HR Department for Carolyn Lattin. She was the one who warned me that I ought to be careful in observing the Japanese customs more closely, for I was not as white as Jean-Christian de La Chevalerie was, and who took me to the Shiseido Nippacho *Mes Amis* dormitory and introduced me to Mr. Kanda on the second day of my arrival in Japan on July 20, 1993. She was the one that took me to the Yokohama City Hall to register my name with the *gaijin* registry office and opened a bank account for me at a Ginza branch of Dai-Ichi Kangyo Bank. She used to work for the E. U. Commission in Brussels, and just as I was, she was hired through a DISCO job fair in Berlin. She handled all the international affairs at the Shiseido HR Department. This meant doing all the paperwork for the interns from France and writing various reports in flawless Japanese. When the top beauty consultants from Germany visited the Shiseido Omori International HQ in the spring of 1994, she acted as the translator. She translated my corporate overview presentation in English to German for the visiting guests. Whenever I think of a highly educated and polished German corporate professional now, I still conjure up the images of Dana Jourdan.

Just as I eventually began to resent Anne Neumann and Carolyn Lattin for taking advantage of their elevated and privileged status within the Shiseido Company, I grew resentful of Dana Jourdan, particularly during and after my employment contract renewal process in the summer of 1994. Dana Jourdan was politically instrumental in helping Carolyn Lattin to secure a dormitory in Heiwajima, only a 15-minute walking distance from the Shiseido Omori International HQ in the summer of 1994, whereas she took absolutely no part in taking up my cause to improve my housing arrangement within the Shiseido HR Department. I could not figure out at the time why she was so unwilling to act on my behalf, but in hindsight, it was highly possible that she did not wish to give any appearance to the people around her at the Shiseido HR Department that she harbored any affectionate feeling towards me by doing anything positive because she has by then already exhausted the tolerance of those around her with the Carolyn Lattin case. She herself was walking on a tight sexual and moral tolerance rope in Japan. This was another major factor that was fueling my resentment against Dana Jourdan in my psychology at the time. She had been engaged to a Japanese national, and her purpose of coming to Japan was ostensibly to get married to her Japanese boyfriend whom she had met in Europe and to reside permanently in Japan. She was no stranger to Japan, having majored in Japonology while in college. Although the two were very different characters, Oscar Godoy and Dana Jourdan both had one point in common in that they were extremely knowledgeable in the inner workings of the Japanese system and mindset. As Caucasians, they were sharply aware that they could bend the rules and get away with it in Japan. More than anyone else, they were keenly aware that the local Japanese rules and moral codes did not apply to them personally precisely because they were Caucasians, so they made the best use of their privileged immunity in Japan. When her boyfriend finally joined her once again from Europe in the summer of 1993, Dana

Jourdan quickly abandoned the company housing provided by the Shiseido HR Department and moved in with her boyfriend in an apartment. This was not unusual in Europe, but in Japan, unmarried cohabitation was considered a social blasphemy still, and anyone found to be engaged in such hideous escapade would be asked to resign from the company forthwith. This was not the case with Dana Jourdan, however. The managers at Shiseido HR Department looked the other way precisely because Dana Jourdan was white employee. So she cohabited with her boyfriend for several months without being married until she decided to finally make it "official" by getting the marriage papers. Married employees were paid at higher rates than unmarried employees at Shiseido. This might sound absurd, but the collectivist mentality at the company rationalized that married employees required higher living expenses. So in order to finance her cohabitational arrangement with her boyfriend, Dana Jourdan conveniently decided to obtain the marriage papers. One wondered whether such an elegant palace maneuver could have been accomplished, if it had not been executed by a white person in Japan. I brought this up with Ms. Ishiwata during the employment contract renewal process. Specifically, I questioned her why Dana Jourdan and Anne Neumann were granted a greater degree of latitudes in their personal lives by the way of privileged housing conditions. Dana Jourdan is now thought to be working at the German subsidiary of Shiseido in Düsseldorf.

Cameron Brown

On the day after the Fourth of July in 1995, I phoned Cameron Brown from Foster City, California. To my amazement, she has just gotten married on the Fourth of July at Notre Dame Cathedral in San Francisco and was ready to leave for her honeymoon in Paris. I called her because I was overwhelmed by the nostalgia of Japan, watching the spectacular firework display the night before. I knew that she was from Los Altos Hills in the San Francisco Bay Area from the conversation I had on the day I met her for the first time on July 20, 1993.

She was one of the original Shiseido Girls. I did not have the prescience to see that she was planning to leave Japan as I was newly ordained in my post at the Shiseido Omori International HQ. A clear sign of this was that she was offering to sell me her NTT telephone bond on July 21, 1993. I did not understand what "an NTT telephone bond" was at the time, so I did not see that she was about to leave the country and trying to liquidate all her assets in Japan. She was an MBA who had higher aspirations in Japan. It is a bit of mystery to this day as to why she chose to go to Japan in the first place. Was she motivated by a prospect of finding someone special in Japan like Carolyn Lattin? Or was she simply too *naïve* and uninformed about Japan before she went there just as I was? It is difficult to speculate. She told me as she was leaving Shiseido that she felt like a personal secretary to Mr. Mori, rather than a mid-level manager that she rightly deserved to be, with her advanced degree in business. Just before she left Japan in December of 1993, she paid a visit to the Shiseido Omori International HQ to bid last farewells to the employees there. Anne Neumann was away in Germany at the time for the annual European marketing conference. Cameron Brown and I exchanged a hearty handshake, and I joked that she was setting a bad precedence for me. Little did I know then that only 12 months after that handshake, I was to follow the exact footsteps that she was taking. She is now married and lives on the East Bay.

Kerry

Another one of the first original Shiseido Girls to quit Shiseido abruptly was Kerry. I once had a lunch with her in Ginza in August of 1993. Also present at the lunch were Jean-Christian de La Chevalerie and Cameron Brown. She was a hard-core vegetarian who sent back a dish that she ordered because it contained morsels of visible meat on it. She was working for a Swiss bank by the time I joined Shiseido. She spoke of Ms. Ishiwata pejoratively at the lunch.

Just as Dana Jourdan was of Carolyn Lattin, Kerry was a close ally of Anne Neumann. As a matter of fact, Jean-Christian now suspects that it was Kerry who introduced her current husband to Anne Neumann in Tokyo. She was a mysterious character who knew a lot about Japan. It was more than possible, reflecting in hindsight, that she had spent some time in Japan during her childhood. More than anyone else among the Shiseido Girls, she was well knowledgeable of how a white woman could thrive in Japan. It would be no exaggeration to say that she was Anne Neumann's best friend. As such, she provided strong psychological sustenance for comfort, friendship and entertainment. It was Kerry's zing for Latin American men that also drove Anne Neumann to fraternize frequently with them. It is no coincidence that both she and Anne Neumann became pregnant by Latin American men in Japan. Her current whereabouts are unknown.

Megan Dorherty

In Australia, Megan would have been just another Irish lass, but in Japan, she achieved a stunning degree of success with her low level of education. She loved plying golf back home in Australia. She spoke no

Japanese, but apparently she came to Japan with a determination to earn as much money as possible using her white skin. I first met her walking with a friend near the Yokohama Stadium on September 26, 1993. I introduced myself and asked her out for a date. She declined, citing that she had to work at a hostess bar. Her initial reaction was very cautious. She said she thought I was a Japanese immigration officer and came to question about her illegal employment at the hostess bar. Tokyo was a small town, and I bumped into her several times on trains and streets. The focus of her conversation at each encounter always was how she managed to be invited to the parties at the American military bases. One such incident took place one night at the end of June, 1994, when I came upon her on the street near the hostess bar where she used to work near the Kanai Station. She received an invitation to attend a Fourth of July party at the U. S. military base in Yokozuka, and she was exuberant about it. I tried to explain to her calmly that those that joined the military back home in the U. S. were considered to have come from the working class of America, and they did not exactly fit the expectations as the most desirable group of men in the minds of young women back home, but such explanation would serve no logic to her understanding of the U. S. service men in Japan. They were white, and that was all it mattered, so an opportunity to socialize with them was golden opportunity for her. The term, "the U. S. service men" was a code name for the Caucasian men in Japan.

Perhaps she was typical of many white women who came to Japan to work, as she had to strictly maintain the strange dichotomy of having to "entertain" Japanese men for work, yet preferring to be with white males privately, no matter how socially undesirable they were so long as they were white. The psychological separation and the limits that they set were purely based on race. So they walked on a very thin line every day, having to be careful and be on the look out every waking moment of their existence in Japan to make sure that that would not commingle with an Asian male in a wrong way by mistake or raise expectations too high in the minds of Japanese men around them. This dichotomy was reflected on their daily conduct and hostile initial attitudes against ever Japanese man.

Along with Amanda Kidd, Megan was the woman that reminded me once again how race played the singular and critical role in Japan. This was proven by her preference for (white) American service men. These young disenfranchised from the heartland of America, who would normally be considered to be to the low-class in the U. S., were suddenly the most desirable class of men in Japan, not based on their intelligence, wealth or moral righteousness, but simply on their possession of Caucasian racial DNA materials and their ability to dispense them.

Several months later, I was shocked to see the nude pictures of Megan in a weekly magazine I found in a bathroom at the Shiseido Omori International HQ. She was pictured hugging various statutes and posing somewhat artistic poses in the countryside of Japan. She must have been paid handsomely, and how she made the contacts for the gig was a mystery. Her whereabouts are not known at this time.

Amanda Kidd

When I think of an epitome of passive racist woman in Japan today, I often think of Amanda Kidd. Amada was from a small, farming town in New Zealand. She came to Japan on a private host family exchange program to learn Japanese. She was no stranger to Japan, as she had previously once resided in the historic town of Kyoto by the time I met her. I approached her at a McDonald's in Shinjiku over the New Year's break in 1994, and ever since then we went out to eat many times together.

Although she never explicitly stated this, she was soberly aware of her superior social position as a white woman in Japan. As such, she did everything she could to exploit her elevated position and took full personal advantages of this fact over me. We went out to eat countless times in Ebisu, Shibuya, Roppongi and Shinjiku, and I was expected to pick up the tab every time. I fetched for her Shiseido makeup samples whenever they were available. I brought her back her favorite perfume from a business trip to Paris in March of 1994. I composed her résumé. She managed to manipulate me into doing all this because she knew well that she had the bait of white supremacy, and she was an astute manipulator of this inequality. Thus, although she was never egregious enough to dismiss me at my first approach, she was racially motivated enough to refuse to even hold my hands. Our exchanges in the relationship were not equal, not even remotely beneficial for me. My relational exchanges with her (*e. g.,* the interplay of requests, ideas and commands) were always one-way, asymmetrical. This meant that there was an uneven distribution of power and unequal valuation of outcomes or benefits[16] because she knew that she could always play the race card in her favor. Because of this, I always experienced negative outcomes with her, and the relationship had to come to an end. Just as was the case with Oscar Godoy, she was highly cognizant of the fact that I was supposed to be aware of my racially inferior position. I played along until it was absolutely clear of her passive racism based on white supremacy. By March of 1994, I could no longer ignore the fact that if I had been a white Caucasian male, she would

---

[16] - Baldwin, David A. "Power and Social Exchange," *The American Political Science Review.* 72 (1978): pp. 1229-1242.

have treated me more favorably and intimately. So I confronted her about this, and she would fervently deny it. She insisted that her previous boyfriend in New Zealand was an African-American professional basketball player, and her parents would rather wish her to find an Asian boyfriend than a black one. I knew instantly this was a lie because I had marked a pattern in my mindset from the previous experiences that white women often refer to their acceptance of a black male as the proof of their not being prejudiced against Asian males, as though Asian males and African males were one and the same. Though they might be both non-whites, they were two very different entities. It was the white racist compartmentalization that justified the notion that they belonged to a same "category." Shawna S. Mund repeated the exactly same catechism in a conversation in August of 1998, when I met her once again in Salinas, California after having once met her four years previously in August of 1994 in Yokohama: Because she did not mind being approached by a black male at a local bar in Monterey, she could not possibly be prejudiced against me. In Massachusetts, women from the U. S. Virgin Island often used to repeat this argument as an excuse to conveniently reject me.

In February of 1994, Amanda found herself a job at a hostess bar. She attempted to prolong our lopsided and superficial relationship by inviting me to her place of work, but by then I knew I had to terminate the relationship. I spotted her a few times after I left her at various locations in Roppongi, but I completely ignored her.

Meeting and interacting with an unscrupulous individual like Amanda Kidd and being gravely manipulated by her evil racist treatment would naturally exacerbate the negative memories of Japan.

Jennifer Harmata

Being lonely and lacking a normal social company of women, I began to frequent a *soap house* or a brothel in Shibuya. The place was called the Garden of Eden, and I was led there by Ryo Yamanishi, my next door neighbor, after a weekend of joking and daring about the place and after having read about it in a men's magazine. There was no way I could have found the place on my own, having to navigate through the confusion and labyrinth of streets in Shibuya. I met Jennifer Harmata at the Garden of Eden in the late November of 1993. She used the stage name, "Lu Lu" there. I found out about this later, but she was featured prominently in a men's magazine once as the most desirable (white) woman at the Garden of Eden. According to her own story, she was a commodities dealer in Vancouver, British Columbia, trading in the Chicago exchanges. She was enjoying a high-flying life in the early 1990's until she lost everything. Although she once drove a latest Mercedes, after she had became too greedy and executed a bad trade, she found herself in a heavy debt. So in order to earn back the money, she came Japan to work as a "model." At least that was what she told her mother. Instead, she began to work at the Garden of Eden. How she made the contact to work at that bordello was a mystery to this date, but what was not mysterious was that she was a making an enormous amount of money. Seeing about 15 clients a day, she must have had about $2,000 take-home pay every day. For the first few weeks of my acquaintance with Jennifer, I was very happy, as I finally acquired, for the first time in my life, an unlimited and easy access to a woman to whom I was attracted. What is unforgettable about Jennifer was that she had a large wooden cross around her neck. I tried my best to befriend her outside the Garden of Eden by waiting for her until 2 o'clock in the morning one weekend, but she refused to establish any friendship with me. Her excuse was that she wished to spend some time with her dog during the days off. Then her strange dichotomy gradually began to confuse me even more. She was not afraid to be intimate with Japanese or Asian males at her work; yet she was not willing to establish any social bonds with them. In other words, she would work with them for money, but would absolutely not socialize with them. I still recall that she strictly forbade me from kissing her. This prohibition probably was the mental limitation rule that the vast majority of white women carried around in Japan, except in the case of Jennifer Harmata, her work involved sex.

I attempted my best to become her friend. I asked her extensively about her life in Vancouver. She told me that her only boyfriend died in a car accident. When her mother came to visit her in Japan, I offered myself to see her, but Jennifer refused, citing that she did not wish to give her mother a wrong and unacceptably embarrassing impression that she found a boyfriend in Japan. Then she demanded that I let her borrow $2,000 so that she could have something to show her mother for. Thus, I stopped seeing her cold turkey. Aside from the fact that she was sexually compliant in Japan, she was nonetheless exactly on the same *modus operandi* with Amanda Kidd, be it at a different tolerance level as far as her passively racist limitation was concerned, so I had to stop seeing her. Just as was the case with Amanda Kidd, meeting and interacting with an unscrupulous character like Jennifer Harmata would permanently alter my perception of Japan. These two women would forever occupy my mind as the evil twin white sisters of Japan. I now suspect Jennifer to be working in the financial sector in the Vancouver area once again.

Kathy Gunn

Being lonely and confused in a far away land in Japan, I was becoming desperate for a meaningful friendship, and I sought for new friends in Roppongi almost every weekend beginning in January of 1994, after the lonely and miserably Christmas break in Nippacho. Roppongi and Hiroo areas were small pockets in Tokyo where young Americans, Australians, Brazilians, Britons, Canadians, Israelis, New Zealanders, *etc.* congregated on weekends. During the day on weekdays, these young people worked as English teachers, street jewelry vendors, bar hostesses and corporate professionals. Just as other parts of Tokyo, because of its maze-like layout of the streets, without knowing the specific address and locations of the places beforehand, finding any bar or disco was almost impossible in Roppongi. Nevertheless, I managed to find a few locations where there was no cover charge to enter. One such place was Baccarat, which charged no cover charge until 10 PM on weekends. I spent a lot of time at Baccarat. One Australian woman that I met at Baccarat was Kathy Gunn. She was craving for cigarettes, and although I was a non-smoker, I always carried around some cigarettes, and I offered her one. She came to Japan with her mother and sister, and she worked as a private English teacher. Just as I was just getting acquainted to Kathy, she had to return to Australia to renew her work visa, and I never saw her again.

Shawna S. Mund

Through the miracle of the Internet, I was able to locate Shawna four years after I had first met her in Yokohama in August of 1994. According to my conversations with her, she went to Japan to see if there were any teaching jobs available four years earlier. She was from a small farming town in Saskatchewan. On August 6, 1994, I had met her at the Yokohama Station, as she was wondering around and looking as if she was lost. I stopped and helped her out. It was a Saturday, and that night, I came upon her once again on the street in Roppongi. Along with her friends, we wondered about the streets of Tokyo until 2 o'clock in the morning, discussing issues ranging from teacher's unions in Canada to the names of all the suburbs on the San Francisco peninsula. Shawna ditched me, saying that she would be staying at her friends', Greg and Shelly Noble's, house. After we were separated that night, I checked into a capsule motel in Sinjuku and spent the night there, being unable to return to the Shiseido Nippacho *Mes Amis* dormitory. Going back to Nippacho from Shinjiku would have cost me nearly $200 by taxi. I was naturally disappointed how Shawna abruptly dismissed me that night. Her psychological state at the time probably was to be as far away from her home as possible, after having just annulled her engagement to her boyfriend. She was a very brave soul in that sense, and I do not think it is a mere coincidence that in 1998 she works as a teacher in Salinas, California. She wishes to be as far away from the place of bad memory as possible. I recorded my encounter with her in my journal on Wednesday, August 10, 1994, in the following way:

> August 10, 1994 Wednesday Sunny
> I was told over the phone tonight that Shawna Mund has mysteriously gone back to Canada, I do recall distinctively that when I was out with her last Saturday with Greg and Shelly Noble that Shawna was planning to return to Saskatchewan on August 24, 1994. She must have instructed the person at the phone number that if I should call, just lie that she has gone back to Canada just so that she could get rid of me. I can not possibly deduce what was prompting her to shun me, except that she was racially motivated. Shawna Mund went to the University of Saskatchewan, was a teacher at a high school in Moose Jaw, taught Algebra, 27, was engaged last year around this time. Her hallmark, however, was that she looked just like Reba McEntire.

Thanks to the wonders of the Internet technology, I was able to meet her once again at the end of August in 1998 in a small town near Salinas, California by contacting the alumni service at the University of Saskatchewan. She was still unmarried. She too had a strong and distinct memory of me in Japan. According to the conversation that I had with her on that day, I discovered that we were out on the same part of Tokyo on the night of Saturday, August 13, 1994, and it was a pure miracle that we did not run into each other again then. We were only one block away from each other. She injured herself seriously on the head that night and had to return to Saskatchewan with a massive bandage. While she insisted that she tried to apologize for abruptly abandoning me and mistreating me in Japan by sending postcards to all Parkers in San Francisco and telephoning me at the Shiseido Omori International HQ from Saskatchewan to express her regrets, I had to theorize that her behavior in Japan was indeed racially-motivated. Just as Holly H. Williams, she abruptly abandoned me in Japan. The sudden abandonment had become a clear pattern of how white women behaved towards me in

Japan after even a slight hint of or display of friendship. They knew that they had to make a sudden cut-off at some point so as to make sure that no further complication of intimacy could result. Shawna now works as a teacher at a middle school in Salinas, California.

Elaine Corbett
On one weekend day in July of 1994, I was wondering around the Sinjuku area to look for a movie to watch. There were over 30 movie theaters within the walking distance from the Sinjuku Station alone. Elaine was also searching for a movie to watch, and we ran into each other in front of the box office at the entrance of a movie theater. She was from a small island off the coast of Vancouver, British Columbia, and she was working as an English teacher at an English school, GEOS, in Seiseki Sakuragaoka. According to the conversation that I had with her, she grew up in a small Finnish community, and coming to Japan was, therefore, a quantum leap forward for her. We saw *What's Eating Gilbert Grape?* together, and as with other white women that I encountered in Japan, she was superficially cordial to a certain point, yet there was a definite limit as to how cordial she could become. We exchanged telephone numbers, but I never contacted her again.

Holly H. Williams
Due the strong Yen in 1993, it suddenly became fashionable for many language schools in Japan to hire white employees from overseas as English teachers. There were many so-called "language schools" in Japan that were catered towards busy professionals and college-age youths by offering night classes all around Tokyo. One language school, NOVA, boasted that *all* of its teachers were white in its advertisements. Thus, many young people from Australia, Britain, Canada, New Zealand and the U. S. were hired as English teachers in various parts of Tokyo. The only qualification, aside from being white Caucasian, was to have a college degree from an English-speaking institution. They were provided with affordable housing and decent salary to teach English to the Japanese. They often had to sign a contract, which lasted typically one year. After signing the contract, they had to go to a Japanese consulate overseas to obtain a work visa. The most convenient and the closest consulate outside Japan was in Seoul. Many white *gaijins* often go to Seoul to obtain work visa so that they can work legally in Japan. On August 18, 1993, I was in Seoul to obtain a work visa to work at Shiseido legally. Waiting on a line, I met Holly at the Japanese consulate in Seoul. She was from a town near Boise, Idaho, and she wanted to become an author. I found out that she and I had a lot in common, as I was working on my first book at

the time. She was indeed a world traveler, as she had lived and worked in Hungary and Czech Republic before she came to Japan to work as an English teacher at NOVA in Shibuya. We had a dinner together at the hotel that I was staying, and we became good friends. Having already visited Seoul a few times before, Holly was very knowledgeable of the local Korean food and customs. She knew how to purchase and what to eat from street vendors and where to buy bargain shoes and accessories, *etc.* We spent the entire day together shopping and wondering around Seoul. I was incredulous, yet happy, realizing that I finally managed to find myself a reliable girlfriend of my own. Holly was intelligent, witty, cosmopolitan and extremely tolerant. When I think of Seoul now, I always think about Holly first. Having been in Japan for only a little over a month at the time, I was convinced, momentarily, that the rules in Japan were different and that I could finally live out my life in full potential as a healthy human being. I looked forward to a new life in Japan with Holly as my best friend. I was dead wrong.

My flight back to Tokyo was a day ahead of Holly's. In Seoul, we exchanged home addresses and phone numbers and promised to get in touch with each other in Tokyo. A week later, I sent her a letter to her work address at NOVA in Shibuya. There was no reply. I contacted her by letter a few times more, but there was no reply, either, so I decided to go and see her in Shibuya. Together with Ryo Yamanishi, my next door neighbor at the Shiseido Nippacho *Mes Amis* dormitory, I went to the NOVA language school in Shibuya one Friday night about a month after I returned from Seoul. I asked Ryo to go inside the school building to make sure that a woman fitting my description was working there as a teacher. I waited for her outside the school building and followed her through the confusing crowd. Finally, I presented myself to her at the Shibuya Station, as she was about to pass the ticket machine. She appeared to be shocked to see me once again. She mumbled and sounded confused. She said something about having found another boyfriend or having to go to South Carolina to attend a graduate school. She declared that she did not wish to see me anymore. She said that I "scared" her. I tried my best to console her and tried to find out why she was suddenly acting hostile towards me. I tried to prolong the conversation, but she said she just had to go. After she left me, I stood at the ticket machine, watching the sea of humanity passing by for half an hour, trying to justify what has just happened. I did not want to think that Holly was rejecting me based on my race – what about the time that we spent together in Seoul? She accepted me wholeheartedly back then. But how would I justify her rejection now? I was utterly confused. But the sad fact was that she *was* racially-motivated. It was the only plausible explanation. When she was in Seoul, she might have been in a festive mood on a vacation and she might have been slightly more racially-tolerant than usual, given the brief time and opportunity that she had, but now that she was back in Tokyo and came to her senses, she simply could not bear the thought that she would have a non-white person as her boyfriend in Japan. To her, Asians were those that she dealt with artificially and pejoratively at work, never to become boyfriends with. So she had to abandon me abruptly.

Holly had delivered a psychologically devastating opening blow to my stay Japan. She set the initial template for all the white women I was to meet in Japan, and she remained in the large part of my mind throughout my stay in Japan. I went to Japan for a better life. I went to Japan for equality. I went to Japan for meaningful and healthy relationships. But what Holly has done to me was an exact opposite. How would I reconcile this then? Was I to admit my mistake of coming to Japan in the first month of arrival and return to the U. S.? No. My expedient psychological solution was to deny that Holly was racially motivated and suppress the memory of her altogether. So I did. Throughout my stay in Japan, I pretended that I had never known or met Holly and never contacted her again. In retrospect, it was almost a miracle that I never ran into her again somewhere in Tokyo, as I have with Amanda Kidd, Christine Morrison and Megan Dorherty. It was highly possible that Holly limited her activities and movements in Tokyo just so as to avoid me or that she prematurely resigned her job as an English teacher at NOVA and went back to Idaho just so that she would not have to see me again in Tokyo. I miss her very much and often wonder where she is now.

Christine Morrison

One might imagine that the racial protocol in Roppongi would be more favorable towards the Japanese and other Asians due its very location in the center of Tokyo. Yet the reality worked quite opposite. Within the pocket of Roppongi in Tokyo, the white Caucasian males dominated the scene as the most desired commodities. In other words, white supremacy was squarely in place there. So all the participants and actors in the theater that was Roppongi performed in concert with the starring role of white males there. As with Megan Dorherty, Christine Morrison was looking for the U. S. Navy service men on leave that were enjoying weekends' out in Roppongi. Her mother must have told her back home not to date any Navy service men, but this was Japan, so the rule did not apply because of the racial factor. The race came first. Christine also worked as an English teacher and usually spent the weekends in Roppongi. There were several bars in Roppongi where the U. S. Navy service men frequented, and I met her at one of those places in

Roppongi in March of 1994. The atmospheres at these places were racially tense. The white women there would instantly brush off any attempt by me to speak to them. I eventually learned not to go to these places.

Christine was tolerant enough to speak to me and to go out with me one night in Omori. I found out that she and I had a lot in common. She was a teetotaler just like me, and she used to belong to a sorority while she was in college. Because I had an access to a Macintosh computer at the office, I agree to write her résumé so that she could find a better job in Tokyo. I never contacted her again after our first date, but she and I bumped into each other a few times thereafter at Roppongi, but pretended that we did not know each other and never spoke. Such was the expected racial protocol at Roppongi.

Anne Drew

One of the most remarkable women that I have met in Tokyo was Anne Drew. She was an avid reader and a connoisseur of the modern American literature. Her favorite author was Toni Morrison, and at the time when I met her, she was reading *The Song of Solomon.* She spoke and wrote Japanese like a native Japanese. How I met her was a remarkable story by itself. On one weekend night in February of 1994, I was standing in front of the Garden of Eden in Shibuya. By that time, I had been denied admission to that bordello a few times because I was a *gaijin.* By then, the staff members recognized who I was and must have circulated words that if I came around once again, they were to demand the proof of my nationality and refuse admission at once. So I loitered outside on the street. Then as if scripted, a drunken man was walking towards me and noticing my presence, asked me what I was doing. When I told him that I was contemplating as to whether I ought to go into the Garden of Eden or not, he declared that there was a "better" soap house nearby. When I dared him to take me to this "better" soap house, he led me through the maze of streets to a place called, ironically enough, "New York." It was located on the third floor of a thin building. When I entered the New York soap house, the man at the counter did not refuse my admission. He did not even ask me if I were a *gaijin.* In the waiting area, there was one young man smoking a cigarette nervously. There was a small glass room on the left side of the waiting room, and women in swimming suits were waiting there to be chosen by the customers. There were portrait size pictures of all the women that worked there with names and brief description of likes, dislikes and hobbies. Anne used the stage name, "Nancy," after the famous American writer, Nanct Drew, and Anne was the only white woman working there.

As was the case with Jennifer Harmata, I simply could not believe her presence at this Tokyo soap house. How did she make the initial contact to work at a place like the New York? Although her income might have been enormous, did she really enjoy having to service over a dozen middle-aged Japanese men everyday? Then she began to tell me about her life story. She grew up in Southern California. Surprisingly, she had *never* had a white boyfriend in her life; as a matter of fact, she had never had any sexual liaison with a white male person in her life! Her very first boyfriend was a Filipino male, and ever since, she had exclusively sought out for only Asian males. She was visibly assimilated in her mannerism, gestures and behaviors in Japan. As with Jennifer Harmata, I tried my best to become her friend outside her work. I urged her to call me and meet me outside the New York so that we could form a meaningful friendship. She never did call me. To this date, I am unable to figure out her reason. At first, I thought she was an unmarried young mother with a child, and she was forced to work in a place like the New York due to the unfortunate economic circumstances that she was in, and she was too shamed of herself to let me know the truth, but she swore that she had no children. She was well-educated person, and with her high level of Japanese proficiency, she wrote out *kanji* flawlessly, and she would have no problem finding a respectable position at any corporation in Tokyo, yet she chose to work at a place like the New York. When I return to Tokyo in the summer of 1996 on a business trip, I paid her homage to present her my first book, *The Netherworld of New England.* By then, she had been reassigned to another soap house near the Shinbashi Station. Apparently, the management that owned the New York had nearly a dozen other soap houses operating around Tokyo, and Anne had been reassigned to the Shinbashi "branch." The place was called, "Shinbashi Orange Box." In this sense, she was a corporate professional in Tokyo, except that her business was in the sex industry. Her current whereabouts are unknown.

Jasmine Bordeaux

There is a famous hostess bar called, "One-Eyed Jack" in Roppongi. Normally I would not go a place like One-Eyed Jack because of the high cover charge and the prices of drinks there. During the summer break in August of 1994, however, I was led to One-Eyed Jack by Noa D'ror who has recently found a job there. One-Eyed Jack had three separate rooms. One was simply staffed with the Japanese women. Another was a casino room where all the dealers were white women. The third room was called the International Room where all the hostesses were white Caucasian women. They were either from Australia, Britain, Canada, France, Israel, New

Zealand, Scandinavia or the U. S. The women were paid by the number of drinks that they sold by engaging in conversation with the clients. Jasmine was Noa's co-worker, and Jasmine caught my eyes for her impressive French braids that she was wearing. I was acquainted to Jasmine by making a bet with Noa D'ror the night before that if I had paid Jasmine enough money, I would be able to get her into bed. So I summoned Jasmine to be my hostess one night at One-Eyed Jack. Jasmine was from California and grew up in Massachusetts.

Through Jasmine, I learned of the Asian Triangle. The reality of the Asian Triangle did not register in my mind until she pointed out to me, and it ran something like this: Near the every major train station in Tokyo, one would often see young Caucasian women selling pieces of jewelry items on make-shift stands. Curious and aroused by the presence of white women peddling exotic items, the commuters would often stop, engage in Pidgin English conversation with the women and end up buying the useless jewelry at enormous prices. These street jewelry vendors were not independent businesses. In fact, these white women were actively recruited from the resort spots in India, Bali and Thailand. There were organized by the Israeli Mafia-like syndicates that ran advertisements there. While vacationing in the Southeast Asian countries, these women would spot these advertisements and would decide to come to Tokyo to earn money so that they could continue to finance their vacations in the Southeast Asia. Because the economic discrepancies between the countries in the Southeast Asia and Japan were so great that one day's wage earned in Tokyo translated into three months' living expenses in the Southeast Asia. These jewelry peddling operations were highly organized. As soon as women arrived in Tokyo, they were given all the merchandize, equipment and housing, and they were sent out to various locations in Tokyo to sell ear rings, bracelets, brooches, rings, *etc.* They would return a certain potion of their income to the company managers that hired them. These company managers, young Israeli men, would also have opportunities to date these young American, Australian and European women, and often times, exploiting their better economic status and for being Caucasian men in Tokyo, they would easily submit the women into becoming their temporary girlfriends. While the arrangement such as this might not work in the other parts of the world, in Japan, just for being Caucasian males, they could manipulate these white women. The number of these women involved in the Asian Triangle reached in the thousands.

By the time I met her at One-Eyed Jack in August of 1994, Jasmine had already gone back and forth between Thailand and Tokyo a few times, and this time she decided to work as a hostess at One-Eyed Jack, instead of selling jewelry on the streets. I could not understand Jasmine's attraction towards vacationing in Thailand at the time, but looking back, it was more than probable that she was attracted to the drug infested and the cheap life-style there. Sufficed to say, I did not win the bet with Noa. In the process, I wasted hundreds of dollars buying drinks from Jasmine. Although I was very attracted to Jasmine, I did not follow up on her. By then, I was well seasoned to the racial protocols of Tokyo, and I knew that there was absolutely no way I could ever convince Jasmine to become my friend outside her work. I do not know the whereabouts of Jasmine now. She might still be caught in the Asian Triangle to this day.

Noa D'ror

Because I had to switch trains at the Yokohama Station in order to reach Nippacho, I often conducted shopping in and around the Yokohama Station, and I became extremely familiar with the neighborhood. I did not know this, but by the time I met Noa D'ror in July of 1994, her life was caught in the Asian Triangle. I ran into her on the street near the Yokohama Station one night. She was selling jewelry on a makeshift stand. Along with Anne Drew, Noa was different from all other Caucasian women that I had met in Tokyo. For one, she seemed to possess a high degree of respect for the Japanese people and culture. For another, she was extremely eager to learn the Japanese language by enrolling in Japanese language classes. According to her conversation, she wished to make her career in international trade between Israel and Japan. Her Russian Jewish grandparents taught her to be respectful of all human beings. She had just finished her conscription duties in the Israeli army, and she was vacationing in India, where she slipped into the Asian Triangle. She and I became good friends, and I even loaned her $1,000 in cash so that she could go and get a work visa in Seoul and so that she could show the Japanese immigration officer that she had enough cash to sustain herself at the airport passport check point. She promptly paid back the money, when she returned from Seoul and found a job at One-Eyed Jack. The most memorable moment of my friendship with her was not the time when I made a bet with her on Jasmine Bordeaux and lost, but when we went to a French restaurant together near the Imperial Palace, operated by Shiseido. It was called, "Cuisine Shiseido." For the last three months of my stay, she was my best friend in Tokyo. We shared many jokes together and exchanged our views on various economic theories.

Noa was also different in that she easily became friends with the groups of people that the Caucasian women in Japan would normally shun. One such group was young Iranians selling telephone cards around the

Yokohama Station. Because of the strong yen in 1993 and 1994, Japan became a magnet for young entrepreneurs from around the world who wished to make quick bucks in Yen. Amongst them were young Iranian men selling tampered used telephone cards for $1 a piece to anyone who approached them. Ordinarily, these telephone cards sold for $10 to $50 each, depending on the time unit of the calls allowed, but the Iranians had near underground monopoly in picking up discarded telephone cards around pay phones, resealing them with modified thin magnetic silver tapes and reselling them for $1 each. Due to the prolonged U. S. economic embargo against the country and due to the large economic discrepancies between Iran and Japan, $1 meant nearly a month's wage in Teheran, so there were countless numbers of young adventurous Iranians engaged in this trade when I lived in Japan. This was often reported in the popular magazines and the TV news segments. They lived in sub-standard crammed housing, ate sporadic and unhealthy meals and avoided detection from the Japanese authorities. These Iranians were most blatantly discriminated against and scorned within the Japanese society as the new bands of criminals and troublemakers. Yet Noa interacted with them without regards to their disparaging social status or nationality. When she and I were walking together, she would often spot them and salute them without any hesitation.

When I returned to Tokyo in the summer of 1996 on a business trip, I naturally searched for her. I stood for 30 minutes at the spot in front of the Almonds coffee shop in Roppongi where I last kissed her good-bye, overwhelmed by the nostalgia. She no longer was in Tokyo. I was only successful in finding one of her friends at a place called the "Seventh Heaven" in Akasaka, who told me that Noa was in Jerusalem and that she might be coming to Tokyo once again. I wrote to her a few times in Jerusalem, but she never responded to my letter. I now expect Noa to be working in the retail trade between Israel and Japan.

Shelly

Living in Tokyo, one realizes what a small town Tokyo truly is. The spheres of activities for a certain groups of people were always limited and the same. The proof of this postulation was that I ran into same group of people again and again in Tokyo. One good example was Shelly. Shelly came to Japan on a private exchange program from Australia. I initially spotted her at the entrance of the Shinjiku Station in January of 1994. I stopped her, introduced myself, handed out my business card and asked her to call me. She never called me, and I have completely forgotten all about her until I ran into her once again at the Narita Airport in the late March of 1994.

I was on my way to Paris on a business trip. Recognizing her, I asked what brought her to the airport. Apparently, this was the day when she was returning home to Australia. Wishing to keep in touch with her, I asked for her address where I could write a letter to, yet she flat out refused to give out any information. She almost became ballistic towards me. From the tone of her voice and the body language, I sensed that she was by then sick of Japan and being spoken to by a man like me. She has developed bad attitudes towards all men in Japan, especially Asian males, for she must have been noticed and approached countless times for her fair complexion and red hair. Meeting her at the airport and experiencing her hostile reactions placed a damp beginning on the business trip that I was about to embark. Indeed, as though she was to set the tone for the entire trip, my stay in Paris and Istanbul was accentuated only by the bad memory of my encountering Shelly at the Narita Airport.

Understandably, meeting a person like Shelly and experiencing her hostility would naturally worsen my perception of Japan and question my social position in relation to a white woman like her. I would realize that to her, I was one and the same with the rest of the men in Japan. To her, I was indistinguishable from the rest. Yet I knew I was different from the rest by the way I was treated at the Omori office by Mr. Arai and at the Nippacho company dormitory by Mr. Kanda. This realization reinforced my hypothesis that I was receiving all the discrimination in Japan as a *gaijin*, yet I was not experiencing any privilege that a white *gaijin* would normally enjoy, both from the Japanese and the Caucasians. In that sense, Shelly served as the catalyst for making me realize the starkly dichotomous racial reality in Japan. I have no way of knowing where Shelly is now.

Two Nameless Australian Women

In a small nation of Japan, one's life was fairly predictable. Japan was a highly illiquid and *un*fluid society where one's life was determined from the moment he or she was born. A person entered an elementary school at the age of six, a junior high school at 13, a high school at 16, a college at 18, found a life-long permanent job at 22, was married at 27, retired at 65 and died at 87. All men smoked and drank heavily. All women wished to be married at the age of 25 and remain at home as homemakers. There were no exceptions. If one did not follow this recipe, he or she was considered a failure or abnormal. Moreover, in a small town of Tokyo, everyone knew everyone else. One saw the same group of people every day and every week. One only interacted with about a half dozen or so of people for the rest of his or her life. It was no wonder, therefore, that one tended to witness same groups of people at same locations quite frequently in Tokyo.

In the spring of 1994, I started to notice two white women at various parts of Roppongi. They appeared to be in their early 20's, and I was tempted to approach one of them, but before I did so, I wished to read her demure and body languages carefully because I did not want to experience yet another rejection similar to the ones that I endured with Amanda Kidd and Shelly. Gradually, I began to notice their presence more often in Shibuya and at various other train stations around Tokyo. They were utterly conspicuous not merely by the fact that they were Caucasian women, but by the way they were dressed: Black fishnet see-though T-shirts and military boots that they were wearing each time I spotted them. I even sat right next to them once by chance on a bench where *Hachiko,* the Akita dog bronze statue, was located at the Shibuya Station. I attempted to engage one of them in a conversation while the other one was away to make a phone call, but she simply walked away. It was not until Noa D'ror invited me to One-Eyed Jack during the summer break in August of 1994 that I realized the purpose of their presence in Tokyo. These two women were working as strippers at One-Eyed Jack! In the International Room of One-Eyed Jack, there were a couple of scheduled strip shows with a Latin theme. I could not believe my eyes as I observed them on the stage that night. I was initially flabbergasted to discover that these two women were actually strippers at One-Eyed Jack, but I was quick to see the pattern of my encounter with these women. The vast majority of my sightings of these two women were at the locations near One-Eyed Jack in Roppongi. All my sightings of them were also during the daytime or early in the morning at two or three o'clock on weekends. I never sighted them during the early evening hours because they were working at One-Eyed Jack.

Just like Megan Dorherty and Jennifer Harmata, these two women's visit to Japan was specifically to engage in the sex industry. They were adventurers and entrepreneurs who understood the strong exchange value of the yen and decided to capitalize on the value of their whiteness in Japan while their youth and the exchange rate lasted. I often wonder where these two women are now.

Patricia

Patricia was a French intern from CARITA, SA, conducting a research on the global cosmetics industry. She was in Tokyo because CARITA, SA was a French subsidiary of Shiseido, and she wished to study the detailed operations at the Shiseido Omori International HQ. I was introduced to her by Jean-Christian de La Chevalerie one morning in the

spring of 1994. Apparently, the HR Department asked Jean-Christian to give her a tour of the Shiseido Omori International HQ. The significance of meeting Patricia was that she made it excruciatingly clear as to how difficult it was for me to get by without a telephone and how lack of a telephone contributed undeniably to the absence of any social life while I was in Japan. After delivering the corporate presentation, outlining the overview of the global operations at the Shiseido Omori International HQ, I immediately asked her for a date. She accepted, and we promised to meet each other in front of *Hachiko* at the Shibuya Station at noon on the next Saturday. She also gave me her telephone number and reminded me that she was to return to Paris on the subsequent Monday.

From the Shiseido Nippacho *Mes Amis* dormitory to the Shibuya Station was approximately 90 minutes on two different train lines. On the Saturday we were to meet, I woke up late, but I had no way of contacting her. I frenetically got dressed and departed the Nippacho *Mes Amis* dormitory for the Shibuya Station. By the time I arrived in front of *Hachiko,* I was nearly an hour late, and she was no where to be found. On the next Monday, I wrote a fax to CARITA, SA in Paris, apologizing for my not showing up for the appointment. I often wonder how Patricia might have interpreted this event and wish to apologize to her. This incident with Patricia also sharply reminded me how being forced to live in Nippacho in Kanagawa Prefecture simply made it impossible to sustain a viable link with the activities and appointments in Shibuya and Roppongi because of its sheer distance from downtown Tokyo. In other words, my missing the appointment with Patricia made it absolutely clear that I could not have a normal, healthy life as long as I lived in Japan.

CHAPTER 7

The Managers
At the European Section
Of the International Business Department II

Japan and the U. S. are two very different nations and cultures. It was inevitable that conflicts would arise between my immediate supervisors and me at the Shiseido Omori International HQ. I was too trustful and *naïve* in allowing myself to be under the command of the Japanese managers in Japan where the rules of engagement and expectations were dramatically different. My immediate supervisors were the products of a different educational system, history, society and paradigm, and they would approach tasks and issues completely different from how I would approach them. Looking back, I recognize now that they were extremely shrewd political operators in every sense of the word. They did everything and anything to ensure their political survival in the company first. It is often said that an American employee always seeks for efficiency whenever possible, whereas a Japanese employee always strives for organizational cohesion. The Macintosh computer scandal was the perfect example of how a same concept was approached from two completely different dimensions. I only perceived a Macintosh computer as a means to improve efficiency at the office, but my immediate supervisors perceived it as something that would destroy the group dynamics and cohesion at the office. Japan is a seniority-based society, whereas the U. S. is often said to be a youth-oriented society. The Japanese respect the wisdom and the experience that come with the age whereas the Americans value energy, innovation and fresh attitudes of youth. These are two very different and contradicting values. A good example of this is that one almost never sees a Japanese prime minister whose age was under 50 whereas it is quite common for a U. S. president to be in his mid-40's. The managers at International Business Department II cherished and safeguarded their seniority at Shiseido more than anything else. Their legitimacy and authority derived directly from the years of their service at the company. I, on the other hand, was operating on a completely different paradigm. To me, youth and energy symbolized the wave of the future. It was, therefore, only a matter of time before conflicts began to arise between the managers and me. Perhaps I was too immature at the time, but the proper thing for me to do was to make a visit to Tokyo and interview them first to see if I would be in fact compatible to work with my immediate supervisors. For it was certain that conflicts were bound to arise, I ought to have taken proactive measures. It was never my intention to quit Shiseido abruptly in a dramatic fashion only if an amicable employment condition was given to me, as it was to Anne Neumann. It was an unfortunate turn of events in the history. I am certain that Mr. Arai and Mr. Takahashi each have their own interpretation of events that took place during my employment at Shiseido from July of 1993 to November of 1994.

Mr. Toru Arai

If Mr. Kanda had been a Japanese redneck, Mr. Arai had to have been a white-collar bigot. Someone told me that Mr. Arai used to be a basketball player in his high school and college days. He was, in a limited sense, cosmopolitan and well-educated. Having spent several years at Shiseido Cosmetici Italia, he was fluent in Italian and was very familiar with all the major cities in Europe, especially Paris. I often sensed that he was someone who was extremely desperate for prestige and status. To the best of my knowledge, Mr. Arai never had any association with Harvard University. He never went there or took any courses or seminars there, yet he had a set of Harvard desk accessory items, and he brandished and carried them around religiously. These included a Harvard logo writing pen and Harvard logo leather-bound document folders. To see him cherish the items that he had absolutely no personal connections to, but simply for their symbolic values and status was, to say the least, comical. Mr. Arai was a heavy smoker. When we went on a business trip together to Istanbul in March of 1994, he was shaking like a heroin addict in need for a next fix at the contract negotiation meeting because he was unable to light up. I definitely felt not only the generational differences, but national differences in numerous ways. Mr. Arai could not understand the core concept of affirmative action when I tried to explain to him when we were discussing a strategy to enter the South African cosmetics market. My position was to find a black distributor in Johannesburg, but to him, this suggestion was nothing but an outrage. Mr. Arai could not understand why I chose not to drink alcohol at all. To his limited knowledge of nutrition, he could not grasp the fact that one could actually choose complete abstinence for health reasons. Even worse, just as Mr. Kanda at the Shiseido Nippacho *Mes Amis* dormitory, he could not grasp the concept of vegetarianism. At the Shiseido Omori International HQ, I never socialized or interacted with any woman. This was due to the fact that an American employee would fear charges of sexual harassment at work place and unmistakably separate the private life outside the office and the public life at the work place. Yet in the collectivist culture, there were no clear separations between the two lives; as a matter of fact, they were often one and the same. Endogamy within a company was a rule, not an exception. Mr. Arai frequently stated explicitly that I was a very "mysterious" person. By 1993, almost all U. S. firms were computerized while it was still common for Japanese firms to use pen and paper in conducting daily business affairs. Mr. Arai knew nothing of computers. These and many other differences eventually turned to misunderstandings, and the misunderstandings led to mistrust. And mistrust to resentment, then to hatred. Mr. Arai probably thought that I looked down on him, disrespecting his seniority at the company.

One of the main causes of my chronic and destructive stress while I was in Japan was Mr. Arai. He was my immediate supervisor, and his official title was Group Leader at the European Section and the New Markets in the International Business Department II. My poor working relationship with him was the source of my daily irritation and anxieties. He tried to conduct himself aristocratically and calmly, but it was not long before he began to display his true colors. The entry in my journal on July 23, 1994 recorded the following event:

July 23, 1994   6:30 PM
Because I could not pinpoint the rationality of this incident and in light of the recent events, I must attribute it to the racial factor. When I first joined the firm, I could not quite grasp the concept, so I simply followed the directions from Mr. Arai, but this night's showdown was anything but beyond any civilized reasoning. The tabulation of Cost-On-Goods (COG) price was thirsted upon me since a year ago when launches in Finland and Turkey had been planned. Since then, I literally have been toiling through it, needlessly each time, at least six times, without finding any use. The last time I had to work on this particular project was back in January of 1994, when I acquired swollen red eyes for two weeks out of stress and working directly under the sun light for hours at the Macintosh computer on the sixth floor at the New Business Department office, right in front of the bare

windows. The project itself involved a task of constructing the price structure from Free-On-Board (FOB) to the final purchase price by consumer, tabulating everything along the way. There was nothing incomprehensible in the process. It was just labor intensive and tedious. I suspect that it is this point - labor intensive and tedious - Mr. Arai wished to thrust it upon me.

Although it has been concluded that the launch in Turkey would be delayed until the fall of 1995 and thus any price construction of the products proposed to be introduced in the spring of 1995 would be useless, I was instructed by Mr. Arai to repeat this project once again. This time it was with the current FOB price and 20% inflated price, and meanwhile he will be on a business trip to Paris. Along the way, I consulted Messrs. Asada and Sugita for the exact format for the final copy, but I must have revised it at least seven times during the ten days that I wasted on this absolutely meaningless boondoggle project from the moment I arrived at the office in the morning until the last print-out I had to make right before this meeting with Mr. Arai and Mr. Kimura and myself for the discussion on this project.

What was antic about this meeting was that Mr. Arai started to scream and yell at me from the moment we sat down without even reviewing the work I toiled for the last two weeks. Mr. Arai seemed to be on an inescapable foregone conclusion that because I happened to belong to a certain group; namely, Asian male employee of non-Japanese ancestry, I was incapable of carrying out the project properly. I wondered if he would have treated Anne Neumann or Jean-Christian de La Chevalerie with the same degree of belligerence, hostility and prejudice under the same circumstances. I had the prescience that Mr. Arai would use this opportunity to simply raise hell with me regardless of whatever work I had done. The latest format on the project was suggested by none other than Mr. Kimura, which I followed, because it made a perfect sense to place the comparative percentages of current FOB and 20% inflated FOB against French current price in the middle of the chart for easier comparison.

The yelling session lasted for a good 20-minute, during which time Mr. Arai indulged himself in relieving his daily stress to reassure the racial hierarchy as to who was superior and who was subordinate, to declare that I was worthless and ignorant for the virtue of my membership in a hated group, and to have a chance to be incendiary against a non-white *gaijin* and to simply hold me down when I urgently had to return to Shiseido Nippacho *Mes Amis* dormitory for an appointment with Mr. Kanda.

I am now knowledgeable enough in the theories of organizational behavior to explain Mr. Arai's behavior on this day. Mr. Arai's right to command came from his formal authority. This type of power derives directly from a person's title and position in the organizational hierarchy.[17] Mr. Arai finally had to let go of his insecurity and frustration on this day because he was threatened by my expertise of having superior knowledge, skills and experience with computers, English and other foreign languages. To make the things worse, when Mr. Arai heard from Mr. Nagai only a few weeks before that my employment contract was to be renewed for yet another year, Mr. Arai could not stand the thought of having to endure his formal authority being constantly challenged and exposed of his incompetence by my mere presence. This combined with his racial hatred of Asian-Americans could no longer contain his anger. Mr. Arai, therefore, belligerently staged this episode. Mr. Arai was a skilled organizational politician at the Shiseido Omori International HQ. Organizational politics is the deliberate "management of influence to obtain ends not sanctioned by the organization or to obtain sanctioned ends through nonsanctioned influence means."[18] He first assigned me to this skunk work described above, which served absolutely no purpose for any future use, knowing fully well that its tedious nature would consume me for weeks at the office. Then he picked up a fight to scream and yell at me without even checking my work carefully. I did not see it at the time, but my bringing in the Macintosh computers to the Shiseido Omori International HQ apparently was a highly politically irritating move. The Macintosh computers were a stunning innovation to the employees at the Omori office. Accomplishing innovation and change in organizations requires more than the ability to solve technical to analytic problems. Innovation almost invariably threatens the status quo, and consequently, innovation is an inherently political activity.[19] My successful coup in bringing the Macintosh computers to the Shiseido Omori International HQ in the spring of 1994 angered Mr. Arai beyond any description, and he had to make sure that my employment contract would not be renewed another year to spare himself from further embarrassment of having to see my political

[17] - Bacharach, Samuel B. and Lawler, Edward J. *Power and Politics in Organizations,* San Francisco: Jossey-Bass, (1980), Chapter 3.

[18] - Mayes, Bronston T. and Allen, Robert W. "Toward a Definition of Organizational Politics." *Academy of Management Review 2,* October (1977): pp. 672 -677.

[19] - Pfeffer, Jeffrey. *Managing with Power: Politics and Influence in Organizations.* Boston: Harvard Business School Press, (1992), p. 7.

success and showcasing of computing expertise repeated. Because organizational politics functions outside the official system, the purpose of politics is to shift otherwise ambiguous outcomes to one's personal advantage.[20] Since the ambiguous outcome was the renewal of my employment contract with Shiseido, Mr. Arai's retaliation against me was the showdown incident on June 23, 1994. I note now that he staged this episode well after higher ranking managers; namely, Mr. Nagai and Mr. Takahashi, had left the office at 6:30 PM. The truth, however, was that in bringing in Macintosh computers to the Omori office; I was never politically motivated. I only had the best interests of the company at heart. I was just too *naïve* to realize the true magnitude of what I had done.

I have felt for a long time when I was in Japan that Mr. Arai was treating me badly because I happened to be an Asian-American male person. Mr. Arai often used to become bellicose with me for the most minor and trivial issues. I never expressed this outright to anyone while I was in Japan, but one of the reasons why Mr. Arai was not so cooperative and eager to buy a Macintosh computer for me when I demanded one, was the fact that I was an Asian male, and it did not sit too well with him that I was more knowledgeable and advanced in computer technology than he was. If Anne Neumann had been the one asking for a Macintosh computer, I was fairly certain that it would have been a different story. Mr. Arai used to tell me poignantly that I broke the "harmony" *(wha)* in the company. Of course, this "breaking the harmony" argument has been used as a euphemism for centuries throughout the world to justify discriminatory practices against blacks in the army, women in universities, Jews in private clubs, *etc.* He did not seem to understand how offensively I would take that type of racist comments. Bluntly said, he was very upset with me because I did not act out the racial stereotype that was expected while I was Japan. If he had been better educated, more tolerant, more sensitive or more receptive, my experience of Japan would have been dramatically different, and my understanding of Japan would have been more amiable.

For the first six moths from July of 1993 to January of 1994, Mr. Arai's behavior was impeccable. Looking back, I can understand why. For those six months, I was paired with Olivier Japiot, a French intern from *L'École Nationale d'Administration*. In the presence of a white male, Mr. Arai simply could not act ferociously, but as soon as Olivier left in January of 1994, Mr. Arai's behavior changed considerably. Without Olivier, Mr. Arai now had a license to be reckless, fully knowing that there was no more impediment and impartial scrutiny of a white male to deal with. His behavior

---

[20] - *Ibid.,* Pfeffer, p. 7.

changed dramatically beginning from January of 1994 until I was forced to quit in November of 1994. The most intense conflict arose when we went on a business trip together to Paris then to Istanbul in March of 1994. It was the definite turning point of my negative relationship with Mr. Arai. Throughout the business trip, I had to spend a lot time along side Mr. Arai, we discovered how different we were from each other, not just generation-wise, but in every dimension of life. Mr. Arai was a chain smoker, and I had never taken a puff in my life. Mr. Arai was an ardent meat-lover whereas I was a hard-core vegetarian. Mr. Arai was not fluent in English, and I was not fluent in Japanese to communicate our deep thoughts, emotions or feelings. Now add in the Macintosh computer scandal back at the Shiseido Omori International HQ, the stage was set for a severe conflict. So he picked on me for everything and anything that I did during the business trip. When we were in Istanbul, I kissed one of the hostesses good-bye on the cheek as we were departing in front of our hotel. Over this, he became ballistic, incorrectly accusing me of soliciting sexual favor from her for the night. This type of false accusation went on through out the entire business trip. When we returned to Tokyo, his behavior towards me changed remarkably negatively, as he screamed, yelled and accused me of things that I have not done with even higher frequency and alacrity. Anne Neumann must have felt the differences with him, too, but in her case, Mr. Arai would always acquiesce to accommodate her because she was a white female. Needless to say, along with Mr. Kanda, Mr. Arai formed the foundation of my negative memories of Shiseido and Japan.

Mr. Masaharu Takahashi

As the Deputy General Manager of the International Business Department II at the Shiseido Omori International HQ, Mr. Takahashi has had his share of tenure in Paris at Shiseido France, SA and spoke French fluently. I admired him greatly for his linguistic expertise and international business skills. Mr. Takahashi was a very polite man. Though he never directly engaged me in any type of negative confrontation, as it was the case with Mr. Arai, thanks to his shrewd office political skills, I do not have any fond memories of Mr. Takahashi, either, and here is why: When the Macintosh computer scandal broke out against Oscar Godoy in November of 1993, the first person with whom I had a consultation was Mr. Takahashi, but as peaceful a man as he was, he did not and could not take a decisive action against a white Caucasian male, even when it was against a utterly obvious unscrupulous act that the white person was committing for over a year, despite my continued begging and urging. The best way to describe Mr.

Takahashi was that he was a Machiavellian corporate political survivor who never rocked the boat, no matter what happened. He was a cleaver man whose first reaction to any office development was to project how the outcome of the event would eventually make him look at the end. His approach to every task is result-oriented. He started from the end result of an event, and then evaluated how it would benefit or damage him. Therefore, he never took any sides on any dispute. He always played the middle-of-the-road stance and went along with the winner at the end. He was playing the time-honored political art of avoiding any decisive engagement. By advancing slowly toward an end, it has been possible for him to progress undetected or at least remain sufficiently inconspicuous to avoid alarming and arming others.[21] He was well aware that if my position against Oscar Godoy appeared to be not gaining any organizational momentum, he could bail himself out by not making a decisive engagement and coming out looking like a winner at the end. Because he knew that the outcome of my case against Oscar Godoy was uncertain, it was prudent for him to simply watch my aggressive efforts rather than take the lead himself. This way, he could get off the ship if I began to sink. Eventually, I did sink; thus he was utterly wise in having avoided to offer me any help.

If only Mr. Takahashi had been more humane and less politically inclined to help me out forthright from the beginning of the Oscar Godoy's Macintosh computer scandal, my current understanding and memories of Japan would have been more pleasant. Yet such was the reality of the corporate politics and life in Tokyo.

---

[21] - *Ibid.,* Cook, Hunsaker and Coffey, p. 449.

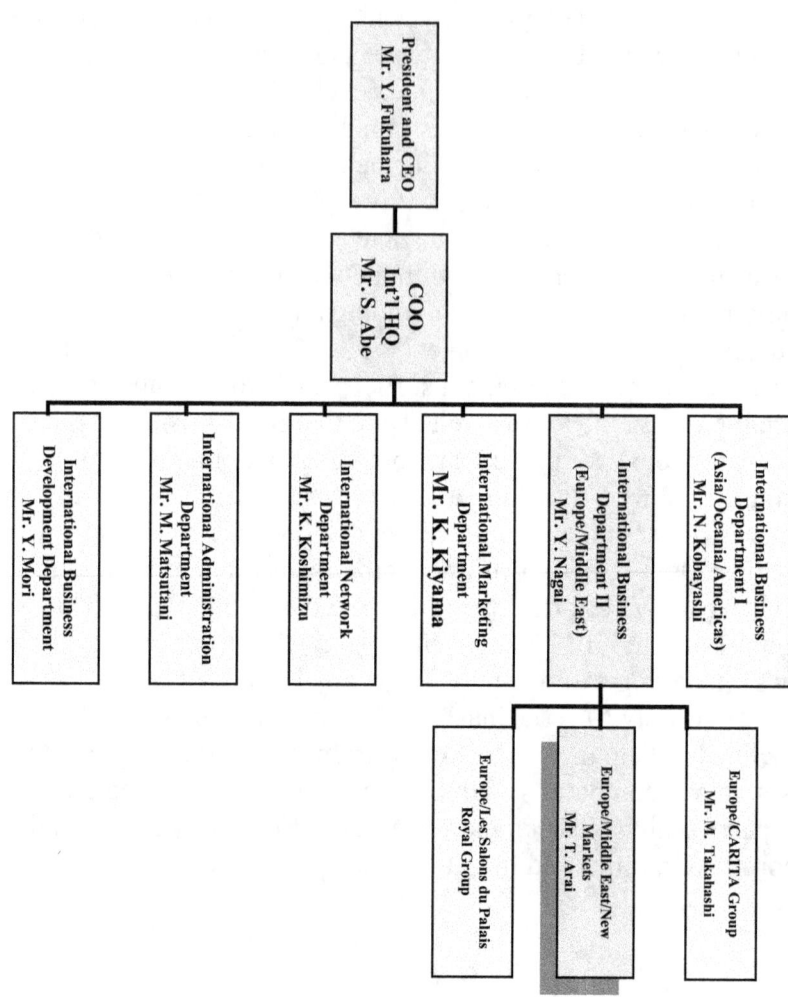

Shiseido Omori International HQ Organizational Chart
in 1993 – 1994

CHAPTER 8

Employment Contract Renewal Negotiation

It is a truism of negotiations that if one side is prepared to negotiate an issue and the other side is not prepared, the prepared side will almost always win that issue.[22] We negotiate to set ground rules for future relationship. My employment contract[23] with Shiseido was to expire in the middle of July, 1994, and as early as May, 1994, Mr. Nagai made an announcement at a weekly department meeting that he intended to make a recommendation to the Shiseido HR Department that my employment contract be renewed, or that I ought to be signed on as a permanent employee. As the General Manager of the International Business Department II, however, Mr. Nagai was a busy man, and he was constantly on the road. I rarely had any prolonged conversation with him or discussed my employment grievances with him because he was always away either in Paris or Milan. When he made the announcement that he was to recommend to the Shiseido HR Department that my employment contract be renewed, I ought to have prepared myself to submit a list of demands, outlining must's, want's and options all at once. Needless to say, having lived and worked in Tokyo for nearly a year by then, there were quite a few. I regret tremendously that I failed to do just that, and I waited until I was presented by Ms. Ishiwata with a draft of the renewed employment contract only one week before the old one was to expire. This was the tactic of the Shiseido HR Department; *i. e.,* not to give a lot of time for me to ponder over the details of the renewed employment contract. Only then, did I start reflecting on my strategies, and I presented my demands to Shiseido HR Department in three separate occasions. I attribute this unprepared attitude partly due to my youth and naïveté, but mostly due to the fact that work days at the Shiseido Omori

---

[22] - *Ibid.,* Morrison, p. 156.

[23] - A copy of the original employment contract can be found in Appendices.

International HQ were extremely hectic from the moment that I arrived at the office around 10 o'clock in the morning until the time that I left the office around 7 o'clock in the evening. There was a little time for me to reflect or set strategies for the next round of employment contract renewal negotiation with the Shiseido HR department. The weekends were spent either sleeping or buying groceries. I simply assumed that things would take care of themselves and that I would be treated fairly by Shiseido HR Department. Although I did not formally write the ideas down, I knew subconsciously that there were some serious improvements that had to be made in order to continue my employment with Shiseido and my stay in Japan. First, the constant and irrational badgering from Mr. Kanda, the residential director at the Shiseido Nippacho *Mes Amis* dormitory, had to stop. Second, the commuting time from Nippacho to Omori was too long on hyper-crowded trains, and I wished to be placed in an apartment near the office in Omori where I could walk to work, just as Anne Neumann could. Anne Neumann informed me that her housing condition was upgraded to the current comfort level when she renewed her employment contract for the second year. Carolyn Lattin also told me that she was moved to another Shiseido dormitory in Heiwajima only 15-minute walk from the Shiseido Omori International HQ when she renewed her employment contract recently. I heard similar story from Diane Hase. I, therefore, expected that a new and improved housing arrangement would be provided for me by the Shiseido HR Department. Third, the incident of July 23, 1994 with Mr. Arai, in which he screamed and yelled at me without any solid evidence of my misconduct, as well as the other minor incidents where racially-motivated irrationality was suspected, could no longer be ignored. Fourth, the hidden cost of living in Japan could no longer be discounted, either. These were never explicitly outlined in the original employment contract, which I had singed a year ago, but they included all types of volunteer donations I was forced to pay (*Vide Hidden Costs for Living at the Shiseido Nippacho Mes Amis Dormitory*), and they added up to a substantial amount over a year. With my haphazard approach to the negotiation at the time I failed to include them, but I should have also negotiated the cost of installing a telephone line to my room at Shiseido Nippacho *Mes Amis* dormitory ($800) and the settlement fee for the Oscar Godoy scandal, which was eating up my mental soundness and causing excruciating amount of stress.

I was thus utterly disappointed to discover that no housing upgrade was included in the renewed employment contract draft given to me by Ms. Ishiwata. The salary remained the same, the housing remained the same, and no other amenity or improvement was ever added to the draft. In other words, I had to re-live the horror of the past year yet another year. This simply was not acceptable to me, yet Shiseido was not about to budge either. I must reason in hindsight that Mr. Shuzo Shimojo, the General Manager of Shiseido HR Department, who was conducting the negotiation behind the scenes through Ms. Ishiwata, was too presumptuous, insensitive and racially-prejudiced to seek out my true needs and wants before the renewal negotiation started. Mr. Shimojo was quick to provide improved housing arrangements for Anne Neumann and Carolyn Lattin, but he did not even bother to ask me how I was coping at Shiseido Nippacho *Mes Amis* dormitory. So when I was summoned to the Ginza HQ on June 23, 1994 at 2:00 PM to begin the employment renewal contract negotiation, it was the first time that I had an opportunity to present my difficulties of living and working in Japan for Shiseido, and it was the first chance for me to systematically catalog all the unpleasant events that had happened to me in the past year. Shiseido and I had an early agreement in principle, however, that I must remain in Tokyo and continue my employment with Shiseido.

Ms. Ishiwata told me to return to the Ginza HQ a week later to sign the renewed employment contract. She instructed me not to reveal the content of the employment contract to anyone as I departed from the HR Department office. On my way to Shiseido Nippacho *Mes Amis* dormitory on the long train ride back, her instruction rang echoes through my head: If indeed all the employment contracts were the same among the non-Japanese employees, why would Ms. Ishiwata specifically emphasize that I do not show or discuss any parts of my renewed employment contract terms with other employees; namely, Anne Neumann and Jean-Christian de La Chevalerie? My deep suspicion was that she was not telling me the truth. That is to say, there indeed was a preferential treatment towards white, Caucasian employees. So one week later, when I went back to the Ginza HQ, I submitted the following clauses to be added to the renewed employment contract draft, instead of signing it:

Anti-Discrimination Clause
Whereas every human being deserves, for the virtue of existence, to survive, to make a dignified living, to receive impartial judgments, to be treated fairly and equally, to be given equal opportunities to succeed, and not to be judged based on a membership to a group with common characteristics, and in accordance with the United Nations' Declaration of Universal

Human Rights of 1948, Shiseido Co. Ltd., will
not discriminate in its hiring, pay, promotion
employment condition, treatment, restriction
and allocation of duties in respect to its non-
Japanese employees based on race, gender,
color, national origin, ethnic heritage, religion,
creed, sexual orientation, handicap, subscription
to an ideology or political affiliation.

And therefore, in order to enforce this
clause, Shiseido Co. Ltd., will accept, record
and register any written complaints in any
language from Pierce Parker regarding any
discriminatory practices, harassment, and
incidents, and if deemed necessary, it will
provide a forum to discuss, address grievances
and remedy such offensive practices,
harassment and incidents. Moreover, further to
this forum, if so warranted, it will investigate,
record, and take due disciplinary actions and, if
necessary, prosecute the offender(s) to the full
extend of the Japanese law.

In addition, I submitted the following two clauses to be added to the renewed
employment contract draft. These two points were minor must's, but were
serious and significant:

Hidden Cost Clause

In recognition of the unique Japanese
social customs, Shiseido Co. Ltd. will
recompense for the expenses mandated to pay at
no fault of Pierce Parker or based on his
individual preference or selection, upon
presentation of proper receipts and vouchers:
These would include, but not limited to,
purchase of new office computer equipment due
to existing inadequacy, donations for marriages,
funerals, retirements, parties, gifts, membership
fees, dormitory fees, natural disasters, office
trips, office amenity fees, *etc.*

Smoke Free Clause
In recognition of Shiseido Co. Ltd.'s current
corporate logo, *Science of Beauty and Well-
being*, and whereas smoking and the second-
hand smoking are the causes of cancer, Shiseido
Co. Ltd. grants Pierce Parker a special privilege
not to be subject to be present at any location
where one or more smokers are present.

Ms. Ishiwata quietly read these clauses, and she promised that she would
discuss them with her superiors and that she would give me the answer on
another date. So the meeting was adjourned once again, and a subsequent
meeting date was set. Although I was not prepared at all for the employment
contract renewal negotiation in the beginning, my resolve to obtain a fair
employment and determination not to re-live another year of horror under the
thumb of Mr. Kanda began to gradually build up, and this aspect of assuring a
fair and acceptable employment contract from Shiseido started to take the
center stage in my life at the time. With the presentation of the above clauses,
the following were my must's:

- Guarantee of my civil rights and equality at the work place. This
  meant no preferential treatment to any employee because of race or
  gender. A follow-up to this was a provision of improved housing
  close to the Shiseido Omori International HQ, just like Anne
  Neumann and Carolyn Lattin, my referent group.
- Guarantee of reimbursement for all the expenses that I have to pay
  "voluntarily" for simply living and working in Japan for Shiseido.
- Guarantee of enforcement of no-smoking policy at the work place by
  Shiseido.

And my want's were:

- Purchase of the latest computer equipment and software to increase
  the productivity; *e. g.,* Macintosh computers and Microsoft software
  products.
- Slight increase, perhaps 5%, on the last year's salary to reflect the
  high cost of living and inflation in Japan.
- Promise of a foreign assignment in another year, preferably to France
  or Germany.

My single option was as follows:

- Permanent assignment to the Shiseido New Jersey office in the U. S.

I regret tremendously now that I did not present all these must's, want's and option neatly on a single sheet of paper all at once. Out of my ignorance in the art of negotiation at the time, I presented these to Ms. Ishiwata piecemeal by piecemeal in three different meetings. This was my major fault in this negotiation process. Shiseido probably interpreted my tenacious indecisiveness and delay in presenting these demands as being insincere and a sign of arrogance.

The summer of 1994 in Tokyo was particularly hot and humid. Traveling to Ginza from Omori during the mid-day's scorching heat was no ordinary chore. I learned somehow that there was a shower in the basement of Shiseido Ginza HQ in the security staff's office. I was whipping my legs and back with a wet facial towel in men's room near the back entrance one day, and a man hinted that there was a shower in the basement! So I went to check this out, and *Eureka!* I began to frequent this shower facility every time I had to go to the Ginza HQ for the renewal of my employment contract. My usual routine was to arrive at the Ginza HQ about 30 minutes before the appointment. Then I would politely salute the security staff taking a break in the room, ask for the permission to take the shower, finish taking the shower, get dressed and go up to the HR Department for the appointment. With a refreshed feeling and a completely clean and dry body inside the dark suits that were mandatory even during the scorching hot and humid summer in Japan, I was in a better position to present myself and in a better mental state to negotiate. I was certain that no other *gaijin* worker was able to do this; that is, to be inquisitive and suave enough to explore the hidden dimensions at Shiseido that were not apparent and obvious on the surface, both literally and metaphorically. I, therefore, believed that I had many strong points that the Shiseido HR Department simply could not ignore, and they were:

- I have already been in Japan nearly a year, and I proved that I was a useful and faithful employee at Shiseido.
- The Japanese language lessons mandated in the original employment contract paid off, and my Japanese language proficiency was better than any other non-Japanese employee at the Shiseido Omori International HQ. I used the honorific and polite forms properly and precisely. I no longer spoke in broken Japanese, and I even passed as Japanese in some occasions! To my delight, the teachers at the Sony Language Laboratory

in Shinbashi gave me straight A's for all the courses that I had taken over the past year. I had attended those lessons religiously and taken the course materials extremely seriously. To the best of my knowledge, no other non-Japanese employee received such high marks from the Sony Language Laboratory.[24]

- I had the superb computing skills that the top managers at Shiseido Omori International HQ had absolutely never seen before. I was able to produce an attractive presentation package with only a few hours of advance notice. I knew ins and outs of MS Word, Excel and Adobe Persuasion (which now is popularly known as MS PowerPoint). I created pie graphs, charts and illustrations in minutes. This was proven decisively and indisputably when Charles Ochsner of CH Project Management, Ltd. in Chiyoda-ku requested Shiseido to deliver a presentation on behalf of the City of Geneva on the merits of doing business in that Swiss city on September 20, 1994 at ANA Hotel Tokyo in Akasaka. Of all the prestigious Japanese firms represented there to give positive remarks about Geneva, Shiseido's presentation was by far the best - it was in a multi-media format. This was something the Japanese audience was not used at the time.

- I also had remarkable writing skills. I practically wrote single-handedly all the daily faxes going to Switzerland, Austria, Germany, Greece, the United Kingdom, Ireland and many official announcements. I seized up the reports submitted by all the prospective Israeli distributors and summed up accurately in a high-quality synopsis report in one day. Furthermore, on a good day, I could type nearly 100 words per minute. This astonished Mr. Nagai. An average Japanese employee usually hand-wrote everything and could not type at all.

- I loved public speaking and delivering presentations in front of a large group of people. I reveled in giving presentations in English, French and Japanese. Again, this was absolutely unheard of in a Japanese company. Even Anne Neumann could not come close to my fervor for public oratory skills

- Most importantly, I was physically already in Japan. I was young, healthy and was full of energy. I was able to make business trips without any family restrictions. I never took any days off. I was keenly aware of the Japanese stereotype that American workers were lazy, so I went out my way to make sure that I showed up at work every day and stayed at work as long as it was necessary into the night.

---

[24] - Sony Language Laboratory in Shinbashi has since gone under, and it has been replaced by another language school group as of 1996.

Despite these strong bargaining positions, I was not able to proceed in the employment contract renewal negotiation effectively because I was not prepared and I had no set of clear strategies. Although these strong points might be considered good aspects of one's employability in the U. S., in Japan these individual excellencies were very much disregarded in favor of the group dynamics and on the merit of the employee's membership to a group (*e. g.,* race, gender, ethnicity, *etc.*). In Japan, what this meant was that these skills were useless because I was not a white, Caucasian employee at Shiseido. Mr. Shimojo was not about to disregard his strong position, power and resources that he had cultivated over the three decades of his employment at Shiseido, one of the *FURTUNE* Global 500 companies, and take my demands seriously enough to re-write the employment contract draft that his HR Department subordinates had already formulated. As far as he was concerned, I was to be treated just like any other Japanese employee at Shiseido. This was his understanding of "equality." To Mr. Shimojo, I was never to be compared against Anne Neumann, Carolyn Lattin or Dana Jourdan because I was not a white, Caucasian, female employee. As the negotiation process proceeded over a three-month period in four different meetings, I began to take Mr. Shimojo's concept of "equality" offensively. I focused mainly on his differentiation of white, Caucasian, *female* employees and me on the first two adjectives - white, Caucasian. To me, his attitudes were outright discrimination. Meanwhile, the old employment contract duly expired on July 15, 1994, but I chose to work without a contract for the months of August and September of 1994 to display my commitment and good faith to continue my employment at Shiseido. Without a contract, I was not to be paid during those two months, yet I showed up at work faithfully and executed my duties to the best of my abilities.

None of my demands for amendments was eventually accepted, and Ms. Ishiwata informed me at the subsequent meetings that the concerns expressed in the three clauses were already in the books at Shiseido, and there was no explicit need to add them on my employment contract. They might be already in the books, but she would not acknowledge, however, that they were not practiced in fact. Life in Japan could be wonderful under right circumstances. One could acquire anything he or she desired so long as there was an infrastructure of informal and unwritten support from the established Japanese society. This infrastructure of support was amply available for Anne Neumann, Carolyn Lattin and Dana Jourdan because of their race and gender. Referent cognitions theory holds that employees are capable of evaluating their work and reward experiences by reflecting on "what might have been" under different circumstances and procedures.[25] I wondered whether I would still be forced to reside in Shiseido Nippacho *Mes Amis* dormitory and to have to endure Mr. Kanda's militaristic regiments and the excruciating commuting distance on sardine-packed trains everyday only if I had been a white, Caucasian, female employee. The answer was definite no. All I needed to look was no further than across from my office desk at Shiseido Omori International HQ at Anne Neumann. Thus, when the Shiseido HR Department rejected to add the three clauses onto my employment contract and refused to act on the concerns that I expressed in them, my final option was to resign. I drafted the following sentences, but did not send it to the Shiseido HR Department because, if there was nothing else, I wanted to win the housing arrangement improvement point in the employment contract renewal negotiation and still wanted to stay in Japan and work for Shiseido:

> In protest against the apparent racial and gender discriminatory employment practice in effect by Shiseido Co. Ltd.; namely, against its provision of special, preferential and privileged employment conditions for white, Caucasian female employees in housing, leniency on social and personal freedom and employment conditions, I hereby submit this letter of resignation effective immediately as prescribed in the employment contract of July 15, 1994 and its amendments.

I made a final firm request to the Shiseido HR Department that my housing arrangement should be improved to the level similar to that of Anne Neumann and otherwise I would quit. I expressed my willingness to work without a contract for the duration of this negotiation because it was patently crucial to me that I sign a fair and acceptable employment contract with Shiseido. My only conscious strategy at this point was to wait Shiseido out. This last-minute botched strategy did not work at all, however. Ms. Ishiwata told me in mid-September in no uncertain terms that in the interest of "equality" in the company, Shiseido could not make an "improved" housing arrangement – because I was not a white, Caucasian female employee. This rejection brought down the entire negotiation, and I had to make good on my

---

[25] - Folger, Robert. "Rethinking Equity Theory: A Referent Cognitions Model," in *Justice in Social Relations,* (Eds.) Bierhoff, Hans Werner, Cohen, Ronald L. and Greenberg, Jerald. New York: Plenum. (1986): pp. 145- 162.

ultimatum, and I decided to submit a letter of resignation on the last week of September, 1994. When the employment contract renewal negotiation failed, I felt trapped in Japan by Shiseido. This was no win-win negotiation. With its superior bargaining position, Shiseido HR Department decided not to provide any improvement on my employment contract. Shiseido did nothing to find out my true needs or wants either before or during this renewal negotiation.

Ghost of Kathy Ho Past

Before this book was written, I attempted to contact Kathy Ho to the best of my ability, but I have not been successful. I wanted to confirm that my suspicion, which I am about to outline, was correct, but without Kathy Ho's personal acknowledgment, the truth would never be known. Jean-Christian de La Chevalerie told me once that Kathy Ho quit Shiseido only once month after she renewed her employment contract "to get married to her (white) boyfriend in America." This explanation made no sense. One does not spontaneously decide to get married in one month with someone who lives in a place an ocean away. One plans marriage. Courtship - that old-fashioned word - is quite organized, even if one does not experience it that way. It consists roughly of three phases: the choosing-each-other phase, the casual dating phase and committed dating.[26] One thinks of the season, place, circumstances and time for marriage. Marriage usually is a centerpiece of one's life, especially for a woman, and it is thought and planned at least over a six-month period.

I had a different explanation. Marriage was a convenient racial euphemism to cover up what truly happened between Shiseido HR Department and Kathy Ho after the renewal negotiation for her employment contract for the second year did not go well. Because she was an Asian-American female employee, she was given a win-lose negotiation, and she decided to get even and to bridge the equity gap by quitting Shiseido abruptly. Just as I did, Kathy Ho sensed the forces of racism based on white supremacy in Japan and sexism lashing their ugly forces in the inner workings of Shiseido HR Department. Because she was a female and because this was Japan, "marriage" was the only acceptable excuse to resign from the work gracefully. In fact, I expressed this suspicion in my racial confrontation with Carolyn Lattin on July 15, 1994. (*Vide* Carolyn Lattin under *White Women in Japan*) The only reason that must have made Kathy Ho to sign the unfair and undesirable employment contract was that without

---

[26] - Dalma, Heyna. "Waiting a man out," *New Women,* December (1998): p. 67.

renewing the employment contract, she would not have been able to collect her last few month's salary in a timely manner because salaries were paid on the following month.

As described extensively through out this book, I went to Japan on an ideological ground for a better life. I was searching for an illusive Utopia. My employment contract renewal experience with Shiseido HR Department proved, however, nothing but the exact opposite. Perhaps, I was too idealistic, thinking that life in Japan would be somehow miraculously better. Perhaps, Kathy Ho made the same wrong idealistic assumption about Japan and learned her lessons. So I reenacted what Kathy Ho had done only a year ago in 1993, just about when I arrived in Japan fresh from Amherst, Massachusetts. I followed the exact same path as Kathy Ho, and a year later, I was forced to renew the undesirable and unfair employment contract with Shiseido HR Department with the insincere intention that I would get even with the company by quitting abruptly in a month's time. So I sent the letter of resignation by mail to the Shiseido HR Department in late September of 1994, only a few weeks after my employment contract with Shiseido was renewed. The price of not being prepared for the negotiation was immeasurable. Financial accounting in dollars and yens could not adequately convey all the hidden opportunity costs that were lost due to the lack of preparation in this negotiation process. Such was the lesson that I would remember for the rest of my life.

CHAPTER 9

Epilog

    Readers would agree by now that the collective experiences described in the articles of Chris Cote, Peter Shepard and Tyler Thoreson were representations of very different Japan and would not apply to a non-European, non-white visitor to Japan. Japan was a very dangerous country in which to live and work for non-European Americans. It was not because there was a high rate of street crimes in Japan. Rather, it was because this Asian nation did not yet possess a strong foundation for social justice and equality. The modern Japan was born in the aftermaths of World War II. It is a product of the U. S. occupying forces that set in places the social infrastructure and the current capitalistic economic system. During the occupation, they succeeded in inculcating into the Japanese consciousness the social values and ideals that were prevalent in the late 1940's and 1950's in the U. S., even down to the white supremacy as it was practiced back then. It followed, therefore, that there was no active understanding of such social concepts as civil rights movement, women's rights and equal employment opportunity, which came about in the mid-1960's.

    There was no conscious and active social awareness to stamp out inequality and injustice in every corner of the society in Japan. Thus, living in Japan was somewhat comparable to living in the Deep South in the 1950's before the Civil Rights Movement or in Quèbec before *la Révolution tranquille.* Although there might not be open Lynching on the streets in Japan, the social infrastructure and organizational behaviors did not take any decisive or preventive actions against open racism and sexism. In other words, there was no guarantee for civil rights for all human beings in Japan. Without checks and balances to sustain a civil and open social *gestalt,* it would be only a matter of time before one would fall victim to the evil forces of unchecked racism and sexism. It would take only one or two people's concerted bullying to ruin one's life completely in Japan, and there was no avenue for recourse. There were no active and publicized national associations for the advancement of colored people, human rights commissions, departments of fair housing and employments or offices for civil rights at municipal levels. I could relate another vignette to support this assertion. One Saturday night in 1993, my next door neighbor at Shiseido Nippacho *Mes Amis* dormitory, Ryo Yamanish, and I went to a small video shop near the Yokohama Station. Our intention that night was to rent a few movies. After selecting a few titles, we approached the counter to check them out. The clerk on duty requested that we open a membership with the video shop and asked for identifications. I presented my *gaijin* resident registration card issued by the Japanese Ministry of Justice, which happened to show my U. S. citizenship. This was the only official ID card that I had beside my passport at the time. Upon seeing this, he whispered something to a co-worker, who was standing slightly behind him. The clerk clearly stated that it was a policy of his video shop not to admit *gaijins* to membership and not to rent out videos to *gaijins*. This absolutely stunned Ryo and me. How much could the videos possibly be? $5 or $10? This obviously embarrassed Ryo, and he was turning red. We quietly withdrew ourselves and stepped out of the video shop. On our way back to the dormitory, we debated the irrationality of the video store's policy. Ryo played the devil's advocate and stated that the video shop's discriminatory policy was probably developed so as not to have any videos stolen. There was a strong stereotype in Japan that *gaijins* were dishonest and unreliable. I argued that the chances of someone being dishonest transcended any nationality. A Japanese person could not return a rented video, just as often as any American person. The video shop might have had a few *gaijins* in the past that failed to return some videos, but I had absolutely nothing to do with them. I was quick to add that there must have been a few Japanese that did not returned videos in the past, but the video shop would never develop a store policy banning all Japanese from joining its membership. It would be redundant to add that this type of experience would alter one's understanding and perception of Japan. Soon I began to notice more openly discriminatory practices in Japan. The signs that read, "No *Gaijins* Allowed," or "Japanese Only" were suddenly more noticeable everywhere in Tokyo, especially in those milieus where sex service or entertainment was offered. (*Vide* Appendices) Inexplicably enough, in those two milieus, the Japanese discriminate against Caucasians actively, openly and vigorously. To this date, I can not rationalize this paradox.

The frustrations and difficulties that are described in this book were not mere coincidences: They were bound to happen in one way or the other. I simply did not realize it early on. The attitudes of those that were in powerful positions in Japanese society were conniving ignorance or just to simply go along with whatever that did not rock the boat too much. Mr. Takahashi's behavior regarding the Oscar Godoy scandal described in this book was the perfect case in point. One would expect to witness such behaviors in the old British colony of India, where a white colonizer could exploit the non-white local population in every which way he or she could with a complete impunity from the authorities, and no one would take a firm stand, in fear of reprimand from the powerful colonial hierarchy.

The stress that I experienced in Japan was immense. It originated from several sources. Poor working conditions from prolonged and continuous exposure to extreme humidity and heat at the office, and the hyper-crowed trains that I had to take to work everyday nearly drove me to insanity. Poor work relationship with Mr. Arai, my immediate supervisor, and the sense of inequality compounded the worsening stressful condition. Stress tends to intensify when a person is alone.[27] I had no support from a wife, family members, or friends, and I literally lived alone at the company dormitory where I was the subject of constant heckling and scolding from Mr. Kanda, the residential director. I never had an opportunity to develop close, supportive relationships that would work as a powerful antidote to stress. Anne Neumann had Kerry. Carolyn Lattin had Dana Jourdan. Dana Jourdan had her Japanese husband. Jean-Christian de La Chevalerie had his live-in girlfriend. But I was absolutely alone. Additional stress compounded because I lacked the political acumen to navigate through organizational politics at Shiseido. Moreover, my inability to develop a network was exacerbating the stress. A conscious effort had to be directed toward building a network. Establishing such relationships would have allowed me to enjoy the benefits of being hooked into informal communications. One of the main causes of my being unable to do precisely this was that I did not have a telephone. No telephone meant absolutely no social life and no meaningful informal communication of *any* kind. Moreover, I was also unable to find a mentor who can serve as a guide, counselor, adviser and coach within Shiseido. I was too busy being scorned, belittled and degraded by Mr. Kanda and Mr. Arai. So I lived in a state of pure misery in Japan.

Thus, going to Japan to work was one of the biggest errors that I have made in my life. Financial accounting could not adequately convey all the damages. First, when I finally returned to the U. S. in November of 1994, my

---

[27] - *Ibid.*, Cook, Hunsaker and Coffey, p. 519.

credit was at ruins. This was due to the fact that I could not send money back to the U. S. from Japan. Shocking though it might sound, no such service was offered from my bank, Dai-Ichi Kangyo Bank. Japan is a corporation-driven society, not a consumer-driven one. This meant that the entire society exists to support its businesses, not the consumers. This would also mean that one could not find in Japan basic consumer services that he or she would normally expect to find in the U. S. The perfect example of this was in the banking industry. The banking industry in Japan offered low loans and an array of financial services to corporations, but it grossly neglected consumers. There were no personal checking services. International payment arrangement was unimaginable. If I were to make payments in U. S. dollars by an international money order, the money order itself would cost $40. This would have been more than the monthly payment for credit cards itself. ATM's only operated from 9 AM to 5 PM and charged extra for weekend withdraws. The Japanese banking industry did not seem to realize the fact that such inconvenience would defeat the very purpose of the existence of ATM's. I wished that someone would have told me about these inconveniences before I had gone to Japan. Second, my going to Japan to work has set back my MBA ambitions by at least three years. Had I not gone to Japan, I would probably have already received a graduate degree as of this writing. Third, I lost communications with Christina E. Guilbert. I had met Christina in Northampton, Massachusetts in 1993. She was very fond of me, and she wrote to me numerous times from Somerville, Massachusetts, while I was in Japan. I regret very much that I disregarded her postcards and letters. In the miserable and chaotic state that I found myself under while I was in Japan, I could not simply allocate enough physical or psychological energy to write back to her or muster up enough courage to realize how offensive such unresponsiveness would mean to her. If I could have an opportunity to tell her why I was so silent and what I had to go through while I was in Japan, she might be forgiving. I, therefore, dedicate this book to her memory.

The most severe damage, perhaps, was that my experience in Japan spectacularly shattered my dreams and hopes. I had gone to Japan with a strong resolve to succeed, but the reality of its social structure simply made it impossible for me to do anything constructive. The disappointment and disillusionment were beyond any description. Likes of Mr. Arai, Mr. Kanda and Oscar Godoy will eternally remain in my mind as wicked destroyers of innocent dreams. Such was the lesson to be learned from the events in Japan.

A Few Positive Points of Living and Working in Japan

In the interests of fairness, I must point out some positive aspects of living and working in Japan for Shiseido. I would prefer to think that the events and dramas described in this book were not deliberate and premeditated and that they were the unfortunate externalities and negative consequences of the Japanese paradigm; that is to say, that Shiseido had good intentions and sincere future plans for me when it offered me employment in Tokyo. I would prefer to reason today that the events described in this book were the results of collective inexperience, insensitivity and negligence, not a premeditated scam. I would prefer to conclude today that it was a noble experiment that happened to have gone terribly wrong. Thus, I also offer some good deeds of Shiseido. On the second day of my arrival in Japan, the Shiseido HR Department opened a bank account for me at Dai-Ichi Kangyo Bank. Opening a bank account in Japan was no ordinary chore. Aside from the mountain of paper work and requirement of supporting document, one must have what is called, *hanko,* to open a bank account. A *hanko* was a small, personalized seal stamp that one placed impressions on all official and personal documents, including bank withdraw slips. One could not exist without a *hanko* in Japan. The Shiseido HR Department simply handed me one. Moreover, I could not have achieved the level of my current Japanese language proficiency, if Shiseido had not had the vision to grow my Japanese language skills while I was working in Japan and to send me to the evening language classes at the Sony Language Laboratory in Shinbashi. Because of my current Japanese language proficiency, I am now an extremely marketable in Silicon Valley. Moreover, because I was assigned to the important market opening duties in Turkey, Finland, Israel and duty-free markets at the Shiseido Omori International HQ, I have gained an immeasurably valuable experience in international commerce. Because of my experience at Shiseido, I am now considerably knowledgeable in the intricacies of international contracts, licensing, trade protocols, processes, laws, regulations and operations. I am eternally indebted to Shiseido for these positive portions of my experience.

In the U. S., a member of minority groups has to think twice before walking into any hair salon or a barber shop for fear of a racial incident or refusal to be served. Haircut is an extremely racially-charged affair in the U. S., but this was never the case in Japan. Although it was a bit expensive (¥6,000 to ¥15,000, which *included* tips), I have never felt any racial tension or been refused a service for a hair cut in Japan. As a matter of fact, I *enjoyed* going to a barbershop on every other weekend. The hairdressers in Tokyo did more than just haircuts. They precision-cut hair like brain surgeons and performed shaving, massage, shampoo, styling and image consulting. I had a favorite barbershop near the Shiseido Omori International HQ, and I kept good relationships with the hairdressers there. They not only gave me small gifts like a brush and a bag of coffee on a few occasions, but I ran into them a few times at Roppongi and hang out with them together there. There were several industries that the U. S. fell far behind Japan, and the hair dressing industry definitely was one of them. I wonder why we could not do the same here in the U. S.

Kobe Earthquake of 1995

On January 17, 1995, one of the greatest earthquake disasters this century occurred in the Hyogo Prefecture of Japan. The most severe effect was in Kobe City. There were more than 6,000 deaths, over 30,000 injuries, and approximately 300,000 people were made homeless. Damage was estimated at over $200 billion[28]. When I abruptly resigned from Shiseido in November of 1994, there was a minor jolt that dashed through the collective psyche of the employees at the Shiseido Omori International HQ. A few employees expressed their disbelief. One such person was Ms. Shioya. On the Saturday before my departure back to the U. S., I was at the Omori office to pick up any personal items I might have forgotten. Ms. Shioya was there, too, taking care of some extra work, and she was attempting to explain to me frantically that there was no discrimination or any preferential treatments towards white employees at Shiseido. I did not debate her. I satirically acknowledged that she was "correct" in a gentle way. Another person was Mr. Nagai, the General Manager of the International Business Department II. After having been notified that I submitted a letter of resignation from the Shiseido HR Department in the early October of 1994, Mr. Nagai summoned me to a special meeting and begged me to explain why I was quitting. The meeting by then was no use. It was too late because he had been too complacent to get involved in my employment contract renewal negotiation process. Mr. Nagai had always been good to me, but I apologized to him that it was simply too late at that point to undo what had happened.

I did not realize it at the time, but based on my conversation with Jean-Christian de La Chevalerie on July 12, 1998, I learned that the news of my sudden resignation from Shiseido sent through minor shock waves to all the *gaijin* employees. My abrupt resignation generated a sense of psychological uncertainty amongst them. All of them *realized* that I was

---

[28] - "Earthquake Kobe Japan 1995," The National Institute of Standards and Technology, the U. S. Department of Commerce, [online], available:
http://www.nist.gov/el/disasterstudies/earthquake/earthquake_kobe_japan1995.cfm

forced to quit precisely due to the Japanese white supremacy racism and discrimination, and there was no more denial about them. This realization alone would not have triggered a stampede of resignations from them. After all, their very existence in Japan was based on the benefits of white supremacy, but only eight weeks after I left Japan, as if scripted by God as a punishment, this horrific earthquake in Kobe stunned the nation. In a small country like Japan, the devastating effects of an earthquake in any city could be felt intimately throughout the country. With this earthquake disaster, the *gaijin* employees at Shiseido could no longer deny the physical *and* psychological precariousness of merely living and working in Japan. The January 1995 Kobe earthquake undeniably exacerbated the psychological uncertainty amongst the *gaijin* employees even more, and now the stage was set for a stampede of exodus. Thus, by the end of 1995, all white employees were gone from the Shiseido Omori International HQ. There were no more Shiseido Girls. The grandiose master plan to diversify the work force at Shiseido has finally come an unsuccessful end.

Sweetheart Deals for Anne Neumann, Carolyn Lattin and Dana Jourdan
      Dana Jourdan left the Shiseido HR Department in September of 1997 and decided to continue her employment at the German subsidiary, Shiseido Deutschland, in Düsseldorf. After brief stints elsewhere, Carolyn Lattin and Anne Neumann are also currently employed at Shiseido America Inc. in New Jersey and the Shiseido regional head office for Latin America in Florida, respectively. How is this possible? Is this a mere coincidence? Or were they somehow attracted back to different Shiseido offices around the world with sweetheart treatments from the Shiseido HR Department in Tokyo precisely because they happen to be white employees? Recall that during my employment contract renewal negotiation process, Ms. Ishiwata pointed out to me specifically that I would never be allowed to relocate at an affiliate office outside Japan. This was one of the key factors that forced me to quit Shiseido abruptly because I foresaw only prolonged misery and absolutely no room for advancement for the future at Shiseido in Japan. If the outcomes were the sole index to gauge the existence of double standard and discrimination, one could definitely say that there was a concerted racial discrimination in hiring back these three white female employees. Shiseido would justify that it is in need of hiring local workforce who are familiar with the local economy, culture and market to run the regional offices. It would insist that it had no policy to send *gaijin* employees back to their home countries after a few years of employment in Japan to work for Shiseido

affiliate offices abroad. Yet that was exactly what has happened in the cases of Anne Neumann, Carolyn Lattin and Dana Jourdan.

If Anne Neumann, Carolyn Lattin and Dana Jourdan had suffered the same misery and mistreatment as I had from Shiseido in Japan, would they be attracted back to its regional offices in different parts of the world? Perhaps my life was less valuable than those of these three white women, and Shiseido was quick to dispense me and would not think twice about the loss, yet it was eager to lure these three white women back to the different regional offices around the world. I often think about my shadow self. What if I had been a white female employee at Shiseido? Or a white *male* employee? What would have been my relationship with Shiseido then? And where would I be now? One of the major characteristics that distinguishes humans from other species is that people have a significantly greater capacity to learn, remember and think about what has happened in the past, is happening in the present, and might happen in the future.[29] Thus, how can one not consider racial and gender factors in answering these questions? I ask myself these questions frequently since those Shiseido days in 1993 and 1994.

In the final analysis, I did the right thing by quitting Shiseido, for I had to put an end to white supremacy in Japan in my own way, but the critical question still remains: Would white supremacy in Japan ever disappear?

---

[29] - *Ibid.,* Cook, Hunsaker and Coffey, p. 172.

Appendices

_____

Pierce Parker
Shiseido Mes Amis Nippacho B-324
Nippacho 338,
Kouhoku-ku,
Yokohama 233
July 4, 1994   81-03-(5762)2307

Tatsuya Ozawa, Ph. D.
1-20-17 Minami-Maioka,
Totsuka-ku,
Yokohama 244

Dear Dr. Ozawa

I must draw your attention to a predicament that I have been experiencing for nearly a year with Oscar Godoy, an English teacher at the Yokohama Research Laboratory, and I must address my grievances against him to seek an immediate [intervention] from you. With your generous [help], I am convinced that this issue can be resolved instantaneously

I joined SHISEIDO International Business Department II in July of 1993. Since than, you and I have met a few times at the Pureness Press Party and other occasions. In July of 1993, I was in a desperate search for a Macintosh computer for the International Headquarters in Omori [where I worked.] Through a contact at my Nippacho dormitory in September of 1993, I was eventually led to Oscar Godoy who sold me a defective and antiquated Macintosh for ¥85,000 with a 3-month written guarantee that a reimbursement be made, should any problem arise in a later date. About a month after the purchase of the Macintosh, I did begin to observe a defect and a mismatch, and I demanded several times in writing for a full refund for the Macintosh from Oscar Godoy. He has been, however, [hiding] himself with all types of excuses, the least of which was that "I had bad manners" and refused to issue a refund on the defective Macintosh.

At this point, I am compelled to file a [small claims] law suit against Oscar Godoy with an assistance from the Yokohama City Consumer Protection Center; however, I have been discouraged by Mr. M. Takahashi [at the] International Business Department II, who [persuaded] me not to [engage] in a belligerent [law suit] in Japan. Since then, I have attempted to remedy this situation through unofficial channels, but I have been unsuccessful.

I [would have to ask] in the strongest possible terms that you kindly assist me in rectifying this fraudulent and dishonest behavior [from] Oscar Godoy.

Thank you.

Yours very truly,
(signed)
Pierce Parker

November 10, 1994

Honorable Walter Mondale
U. S. Ambassador
U. S. Embassy
10-1, Akasaka
1-Chome
Minato-ku
Tokyo, Japan

RE: Registration of Complaint against SHISEIDO Co. Ltd.'s Discriminatory Employment Practices

Dear Mr. Ambassador,

I must draw your attention to the horrifying experience I have had with SHISEIDO Company Limited located at 7-5-5 Ginza, Chuou-ku, Tokyo 104-10. I attended an organized career forum in November of 1991 in Boston, and I was subsequently offered an employment from SHISEIDO in spring of 1992 after an extensive interview. In acceptance of the employment offer from SHISEIDO, I moved to Japan in July of 1993, and I have been under its employment until October of 1994 when I had to terminate the employment contract.

I am a male U. S. citizen of an Asian ancestry, and in the recruiting class of 1993 at SHISEIDO, there were six other non-Japanese citizens, of which there were one white female German citizen; one white male French citizen, two white female U. S. citizens and two Asian female U. S. citizens of Japanese ancestry. I was the only Asian male U. S. citizen of non-Japanese ancestry. There was another white female U. S. citizen, from the previous recruiting class at SHISEIDO, who was from the state of Michigan.

The testimonial I am about to make is regarding the blatant discriminatory employment practice of SHISEIDO based on race and gender, which I suffered while I was under its employment in Japan, especially in housing and at its International Division office in Omori, Tokyo.

Foremost, it must be reported that SHISEIDO was providing an overtly preferential treatment toward white Caucasian female employees simply because of their race and gender. For example, a white female employee has been doled with the most modern portable personal computer purchased by SHISEIDO for her own use, while I was forced to buy my own out of my pocket at 85,000 yen. For another, she was not only exempted from such menial traditional Japanese female office duty as serving drinks to other co-workers and visitors, but she was systematically and deliberately never assigned to any labor-intensive or detail-oriented task. In addition, despite its appearance of bordering on gross misappropriation and abuse of system, she was pampered with free trips to London and New York where she was allowed stay at one of the most luxurious and exclusive hotels at company expenses whenever there was a slightest opportunity. She was also awarded with free trips to Scandinavia every third month where she was the area co-ordinator. On February 21, 1993, the staff members at the International Business Department II (IBD II) were even asked to halt their work just so as to celebrate a little office birthday party in her name, organized by Mr. T. Arai, the Director of IBD II while I was at SHISEIDO. No other employee at SHISEIDO was showered with these types of perks, privileges, and sweetheart special treatments.

On the paramount note, it must be argued that Mr. Arai of IBD II was the indisputable champion of open hostility and cruel discriminatory management practices. While he would display absolutely no belligerence towards white employees, he would inevitably complain about my performance, even if a given task was carried out correctly simply because of my race and gender. Of the numerous bitter incidences, for instance, one evening in June of 1994, I was publicly declared an idiot and yelled at for not having been able to properly compile a price comparison list for the Turkish market. For example, it was determined by that time that Shiseido's launch in Turkey would be delayed another year due to the economic downturn there, and there was irrefutably no use for a price comparison at that stage, yet I was forced to perform this labor-intensive project for two weeks; and for another example, a careful tabulation subsequently revealed that there was nothing inherently wrong with my work.

The most abhorring act of discrimination, however, was the fact that SHISEIDO fully subsidized this white female employee's housing within a brief walking distance from the office in Omori so that she needed not suffer through the excruciating commuting congestion everyday simply because she was a white Caucasian female. Other non-Japanese employees were housed in private apartments where SHISEIDO mostly subsidized, and I was the only

non-Japanese employee required to reside at a company dormitory in Yokohama because of my race and gender.

From this SHISEIDO Nippa dormitory in Yokohama, I was forced to endure at least 90 minutes of excruciating rush hour commute by train every day. This company dormitory was managed by one Mr. Kanda who spoke absolutely no English. In my early months of residence in Japan, I had to simply reply yes or *hi* to everything he shouted and screamed at me in vehemently vocal Japanese due to the lack of my Japanese proficiency, but as the months passed and as I began to understand the Japanese language better, I started to suspect that he derived some type of a perverted pleasure out of engaging me in verbal confrontations in Japanese, fully knowing that he would always be able to degrade and humiliate me no matter what the reality might have been simply because my Japanese was not up to par with his and because of my race and gender. He would engage in shouting and bellowing at me in Japanese with the most mundane and trivial issues. For example, in one evening in May of 1994, I was severely reprimanded and humiliated for putting out old newspapers for the next day's garbage pick-up and not following his own rule of doing so only during the designated early hours of the garbage pick-up date. In this particular evening, I was fresh from a long international air flight on an overseas company business trip, and I suspected that I would not be able to wake up early on the subsequent day in time for the designated garbage pick-up hours.

In reality, Mr. Kanda was not a dormitory manager *(kanri-in)* at the SHISEIDO Nippa dormitory in Yokohama, but was empowered as a concentration camp commandant who could bestow on me any type of atrocity with a full impunity. He not only treated me like a war prisoner, but he had a flagrant and grotesque disregard [for] my civil liberty, human rights, comfort, or privacy. He would often enter and exit my room without any permission, and he would frequently bang on my door early in the morning hours just so to wake me up to agitate me with what I have supposedly done wrong in his eyes. The most inhumane and demeaning practice, furthermore, was the fact that SHISEIDO Human Resources Department commissioned Mr. Kanda to file a monthly behavior report on me as though I was an experimental laboratory animal. Lacking any serious topics to record, he would then document such nonsensical points as my not remembering to lock or unlock my room door, common bathroom door, windows, how I would eat too much at the cafeteria, etc. He often dictated to micro-manage my every behavior in dressing, eating, and sleeping. I was the only non-Japanese employee placed under this type of prison-like living arrangement because of my race and gender.

[By] the way of illustrating another overbearing and over-demanding example, on one morning after a strong typhoon in September of 1994, I was awaken by his loud [banging] on my door which was followed by his humiliating barking and exclaiming at me for keeping the bathroom window unlock. Apparently, the powerful wind from the storm forced it open and a rain puddle was formed on the bathroom floor. Without any solid, scientific evidence, investigation, or a probable cause as to who actually might have been responsible, and although such an accident would have been certainly expected to take place after a heavy rain, I was undoubtedly blamed for the natural disaster, which was no fault of my own, and I was conveniently used as a psychological scapegoat

At this SHISEIDO Nippa dormitory, there was no running hot water in the rest room, and I had to ignite a small portable gas heater. Moreover, with its high humidity and scorching heat in the summer of 1994, the rest room was suffocating with the odor of ammonia and lack of ventilation, yet every time I opened the window, he would dash up to the third floor where I resided just to close the window *even if* I was still inside using the restroom. I lost the count on the number of times when he accused me of not turning off the gas heater in the rest room even if anyone of five other residents on the third floor might have forgotten about it. Every time I was in the restroom, he would embark on a concentration camp-style hawking patrol just to monitor what I did there.

In the name of "group security," reminiscent of a totalitarian dictator, he would often hide or throw away my personal items if I should happen to leave anything outside my room. During my 15 months of residence at the SHISEIDO Nippa dormitory, I lost two bath towels, one coffee dripper, one facial towel and numerous other items simply because I forgot to take them back to my room, and if I should [ask] him about these, he would simply play conniving ignorance of them. Had he simply left them alone a bit longer as they laid, they would have been eventually retrieved.

Another one of his excuses for frequent combatant behaviors towards me was on the issue of the common laundry room where all 90 residents were allowed to use. He would irrationally accuse me of leaving my laundry there whether the items actually belonged to me or not. Because of this, I in return painstakingly had to go on a patrol to the laundry room just to ascertain that laundry was properly and promptly picked up by all those who utilized the common facility.

On November 8, 1994, the day of my departure back to the U. S., he again drummed on my door to remind me in the early morning to surrender the key and get out of the premise quickly. He then made an announcement in loud Japanese that he would now be able to sleep in peace for I would no longer be there.

Although I had communicated this malicious behaviors of Mr. Kanda and the discriminatory interpretation of my living arrangement and other events to Ms. M. Ishiwata of SHISEIDO Human Resources Department, she would forthright deny existence of any discrimination or misdeeds by the company and refused to [change] my living and employment condition up to the level equal to or comparable to those of other white female Caucasian employees at SHISEIDO. No other foreign employee was subject to reside or work under such a degrading environment.

In conclusion, in light of this allegation, I would like to beseech in the most strenuous terms that an official protest be filled against SHISEIDO and warn other U. S. citizens of its discriminatory practices until such time as it complies with the appropriate U. S. Civil Rights regulations.

I would very much like to request that an appropriate action be forthwith taken by the U. S. Embassy against this firm.

I thank you.

Yours very truly,
(signed)
Pierce Parker

TO: Monica Lennie

Dear Monica,

Office politics set aside, we, the employees at the Tokyo office, must convey you of the rest of the story regarding Anne Neumann, as you seemed to have been only exposed to the surface of the matter. It is true that she was once featured in a DISCO employment catalog as a part of the cover story, and no one can deny the fact that she is a sound person with good work ethics. But this is the rest of the story.

It so happened that she is one of the few white female workers in the Tokyo International Division. And as such, she has been showered with comforts, perks and privileges that are unimaginable for an average Japanese worker: She was awarded with an apartment by the company near the office within the walking-distance so that she needed not go through the rush hour hell in the morning and evening while everybody else has to, and you know how astronomically expensive the apartment rent is in Tokyo. Every time there is any meeting or conference, she is, without exception, showcased as the proof of Shiseido's worthiness and status. One white face amongst the sea of Asians would always serve as the living proof that Shisiedo is indeed an international cosmetics firm. She commands, dictates and orders around other Japanese managers, who are old enough to be her parents and grandparents at the office, and she is never challenged and confronted with her unacceptable bad manners, misconduct or mistakes because of her race and gender.

The purpose of this anonymous letter, however, is not to nag on how she is treated by the company, but to point out the unethically opportunistic nature of her *modus operati* and how some of us here are questioning whether her trip to New York City is nothing but an abuse of the system and company funds. According to the honor-based nature and goodwill understanding of human relations, the Japanese usually do not express their dissatisfaction or resentment openly, but a lot of us here are presently wondering if there were indeed a justifiable ground for Anne Neumann's visit [to] New York City at [the] company expense.

Notwithstanding that she is a white female employee, no other average Japanese worker with the same seniority or experience would ever enjoy this [type of] privilege, and we believe that there is absolutely no need for her to take a grand tour of New York City at [the] company expense.

We would wonder if you should roll out a red-carpet welcome in light of this revelation. The decision is up to you, but we are simply feeding you the rest of the story, as Paul Harvey would say.

EMPLOYMENT CONTRACT

This Employment Contract is made and entered into on the 16 day of July, 1993 between SHISEIDO Company Ltd., of Tokyo (hereinafter referred to as (A)) and Mr. Pierce Parker, domiciled at 176 Acacia Avenue, San Bruno, California, USA (hereinafter referred to as (B)).

Interpretation; In this Contract, words in the singular shall be construed as words in the plural and vice versa where the context requires.

1. Assignment
(B) will be a member of International Operations Division of (A).

2. Period of Employment
Employment of (B) will be effective as of July 16, 1993 and will expire on July 15, 1994.

3. Wages
3-1. (A) will pay monthly to (B) for the amount of 312,000 yen (before taxes and social contribution) on every 25th day of the month. However, in the event (B) cancels this Contract during its term, (A) will pay the wages due from the first day of the month to the date (B) leaves the service of (A).

3-2. (B)'s hourly wage shall be 1,950 yen, and in the case (B) works more than monthly working hours (A) designated, (A) shall pay the 25% increased hourly wage as an overtime pay on workdays to (B).

3-3. In the case (B) will be absent from (A)'s working day, deduction of 15,600 yen per day (hourly wage, 1,950 yen, multiplied by eight (8) hours) from monthly salary shall be made by (A).

3-4. (A) shall bear any taxes and legal insurance fees levied on (B)'s income under this Contract by the Japanese Government or any other competent authorities, such as income tax, local income tax, and social contribution.

Monthly social contribution	
National health insurance	8,313 yen
Welfare pension insurance	19,210 yen
Welfare pension fund	5,440 yen
(this amount will change according to the law revision)	

3-5. (A) shall not pay the bonus to (B).

3-6. (A) shall pay retirement benefit in accordance with the retirement benefit regulation set forth by (A), in the case (B) will retire by termination of the Contract.

3-7. (A) will pay (B) commuting expense between (B)'s residence in Japan and (A)'s office.

4. Working Hours
Working hours shall be from 8:30 to 17:30 (actual working hour eight (8) hours plus one (1) hour break from 11:50 to 12:50). (B) shall work the monthly working hours designated by (A); however, (B) will retain the right to adopt "Flexible Time System" with core working hour from 10:00 to 15:00.

5. Working Calendar and Paid Holiday
5-1. (B) will observe and work in accordance with (A)'s work calendar and its regulation:

annual holiday	125 days
annual paid holiday for the first one year	10 days

To use the paid holidays, advance approval from (A) is needed.

5-2. In case this Contract is terminated, no reimbursement will be made by (A) to (B) for any unused paid holidays.

5-3. In case this Contract is renewed and (B) still keeps unused paid holidays of the former year, the unused paid holidays can be carried over only for the coming one year. No reimbursement will be made by (A) to (B) for unused paid holidays.

6. Housing Allowance
6-1. (A) will provide (B) a company house for nonmarried person. However, according to the regulation set forth by (A), (B) shall pay a monthly rental of 13,000 yen.

6-2. (B) shall agree to pay such expense like electricity, gas, water supply, telephone installation and telephone.

7. Job Description
(B) is expected to use (B)'s professional skill, expertise and knowledge in rendering (B)'s services to (A) and to perform (B)'s duties efficiently and diligently. The job descriptions given to (B) from time to time are not to be taken as restrictive and (B) will be expected to make full use of (B)'s

capabilities as an employee when the occasion demands, even though this might exceed the bounds of the job description in force at the time.

8. Air Fare and Moving Costs
(B)'s air-tickets (economy class) needed for enrollment in (A) and return to (B)'s home country due to expiration of (B)'s Employment Contract shall be paid by (A). (A) shall also pay (B)'s moving costs from Japan to (B)'s destination upon presentation of the vouchers to (A). However, in the event cancellation of the Contract is made within one year by (B), airfare and moving costs should be paid by (B).

Moving costs are limited as follows:
* Air freight for unaccompanied goods not exceeding 20 Kg
* Transport expense covering sea-mailed goods not exceeding the size of 300 cft.

9. Temporary Repatriation
In the event that (B) is employed at (A) for more than two years and wishes to maintain an Employment Contract, (A) will supply a return air-ticket (economy class) only for temporary repatriation. In this case, (B) shall obtain a prior approval from general manager of (B)'s department. This temporary repatriation will be considered a part of (B)'s paid vacation days.

10. Termination and Cancellation of the Contract
10-1. This contract will expire automatically on July 15, 1994.

10-2. In the event that (A) needs (B), and further (B) desires to maintain the Contract with (A), this Contract can be revised.

10-3. (A) will not extend this Contract, in case (B) does not reach the performance level, which is asked by (A).

10-4. This Contract can be terminated during its term, provided either party gives one-month prior written notice to the other party.

10-5. In the event of breach of this Contract by (B) for any reason, including but not limited to misconduct, illegal act or non-observance of the obligations hereunder, (A) reserves the rights to terminate this Contract forthwith. In such case of termination, all the rights of (B) under this Contract described will become void forthwith.

11. Language Skill
(A) will not maintain the Contract in any case (B) does not reach the Japanese language level, which is asked by (A).

12. Observance of Secrecy
(B) shall observe secrecy in relation to any information concerning business and technology which becomes known to (B) in the course of the performance of (B)'s duties and shall not disclose such information to any third party. This obligation will continue in force after the expiration or the termination of this Contract unless or until such information passes into the public domain, other than by breach of this Article by (B).

13. Corporate Regulation
Unless otherwise specified in this Contract, (B) will agree to observe the rules and regulations set forth by (A).

14. Applicable Laws
The terms of this Contract and its execution hereunder will, in all respect, be governed by the laws of Japan.

IN WITNESS WHEREOF, the parties hereto have hereunder set their hands:
-

Date: Date:

SHISEIDO Co. Ltd.,

Shuzo Shimojo   Pierce Parker
General Manager
Personnel Department

"American Gigolo"
By Tyler Thoreson
From Swing Magazine

And I thought it was my cologne. It turned out to be the butter. In Japan last fall I was what the Japanese call a *batakusai,* a "butter stinker." The word is relic of prewar Japan when no one ate dairy products and foreigners (*"gaijin"*) were thought to smell like cheese fries. I can imagine the fetid, milky odor that enshrouds an overconsumer of dairy foods, and I would not expect it to attract a lot of women. Luckily, I was wrong. Because I have been to Tokyo, and I am here to say that there is a place on this earth where I am wanted.

In New York, were I live, I am not considered an especially stunning specimen of maleness. Mildly attractive, at times, maybe, but I lack the traffic-stopping looks that seem necessary to garner even a second of eye contact with the beautiful women in my neighborhood. They spot me from afar, a conspicuously unattached male with tight jeans and an agenda. Just as our eyes meet, there appears across the street a drifting piece of refuse, a dog pissing on a Ferrari, anything to deflect the fleeting bliss of her attention. Or worse, yet, she just glides right past with a set jaw and her nose in the air. After these encounters I usually find myself waiting in an ATM line, seeking electronic confirmation that I do, in fact, exist.

This was not the case in Japan, where I worked for a few months as a paralegal for an American law firm. I am nowhere near as beautiful as the man Japanese women call "Brad-o Pitt-o," but I am 6 feet 5 inches and blond, and in Tokyo my Nordic look was enough to win me a little extended eye contact here and there. With the help of a good shirt, that is. Japanese women (maybe women in general, who knows) are suckers for a good shirt. It sends the signal that you are damn serious about looking good, and more important, it appears that willingness to spend money on your exterior speaks volumes for the contents of your interior. It's true. Never, never question this rule.

The proper attire combined with my surplus height and blondness to create a synergistic effect; I would go to clubs and come home with, at the bare minimum, a telephone number. I handed out so many business cards I had to have more printed. Feeling an unprecedented sense of confidence, I brazenly turned my music hobby into a career, announcing myself on my calling card as a "studio musician to the stars." I became increasingly aggressive, asking women to drinks, dinner, a swim back at my hotel.

Sometimes they just invited themselves. Take the women who worked at Trader Vic's, a hotel restaurant my friends and I frequented. We were on fat expense accounts and spent every yen we could at the place, intriguing some of the women who worked there. Two weeks after our expense accounts were changed to a per diem chunk of cash and we realized that less spending meant more money (amazing concept), we quit going to Trader Vic's. Then late one night, I received a phone call. Ayaka and Akiko were shyly wondering why I never came by anymore. I suddenly felt ashamed for taking my meals at Shakey's, and twenty-four hours later, I had a date. With both of them – and a few of their friends. I'll never forget sitting at a table at a place called "Bar, Isn't It?", surrounded by gorgeous women, trying to talk over a deafening techno version of "Smells Like Teen Spirit," when Ayaka decided to let me in one a little secret: Akiko was a-VAIL-able. How wonderfully subtle they were.

The language barrier might have posed a problem – my Japanese never advanced much past a few common pleasantries and the phrase "nice pants," which was helpful on only a few occasions. But it hardly seemed to matter. I was never short of companionship.

Perhaps it is because they liked me better, but I find Japanese women to be extremely appealing. I have not fallen for the vile cliché about the submissive, mysterious Japanese sex slave that causes so many misguided American men to join the Marines. The young, single women I knew in Japan were smart, assertive, and even ironical. And I miss them.

Returning to New York has required a sudden and bruising ego adjustment. There is still plenty of trash floating the side streets, still an abundance of pissing dogs, still plenty to the women who strut past my lonely gaze.

Re-printed with a permission from the author. Tyler Thoreson has written for several national magazines, including *Swing, Gadfly, Salon* and *Lingua Franca.* He is currently an online editor for the *Saint Paul Pioneer Press.* He lives in Minneapolis, Minnesota.

Fond Memories of Life with a Host Family
By Peter Shepard

    I first came from Australia, my home country, to the Eurocentre Kanazawa in the fall of 1991. Although this was my first experience with Eurocentre, I was no stranger to Japan, having lived for three months in Tokyo the previous year and also, before that, making 24 short visits, of a few days only, to various parts of the country from 1983 – 1987 in my previous capacity, before retirement, as a ship's captain in the Australian Merchant Marine. It was during this period that I developed my great interest in and love for Japan, its people, its culture and in general, all things Japanese. The idea of improving my Japanese at a school in the historic city of Kanazawa and living with a Japanese family for eight weeks appealed to me greatly, so I signed myself up with Eurocentre's agent here in Australia.

    However, as the time for my visit approached I became slightly apprehensive, as I began to wonder how everything would work out, what kind of people my host family would be and whether I would be able to fit in with their way of life – whether they were old or young, very formal or informal, etc. Although I am no longer young myself (being 61 at the time), I felt that I would be able to relate better to people a little younger than myself. My instructions from Eurocentre were to take the bus in from Komatsu Airport to Kanazawa Station (about 30 km), phone my host family, then take a taxi out to their place (Eurocentre had supplied the name and address). As I entered the airport arrival lounge, a young woman approached and asked if I was "Shepardo-san." My first thought was that she was from Eurocentre and how nice it was of them to have someone come all this way to meet me on a Sunday afternoon. However, when I said that I was indeed Shepardo, she replied that she was Hattori, my host "mother' and then introduced me to "oto-san," my host "father." I judged Mr. Hattori to be in his early forties and Mrs. Hattori to be in her mid-thirties, although even today, I am still not sure their exact ages.

    Right from that very moment, I realized what nice people they were and began to feel at ease. Having previously lived in Tokyo, I took an interest in the type of housing in the small towns and villages through which we drove on the way from the airport to their home. Houses appeared much larger and of better quality than I was used to in Tokyo and many had gardens around them. I wondered what the Hattori's house, my future home, was going to be like. I need not have worried.

    From the moment I arrived, I was delighted with everything. The house was large and modern, the interior a comfortable blend of Japanese and

Western styles. I was quite pleased to find that I was not going to be the only Eurocentre student there, as Andrew Cacciatore from Yonkers, New York, had arrived a few hours before me. Neither of us spoke Japanese very well at that time, but by pooling our meager expertise and working together, we were able to make quite a good combination. Despite this, at times, our conversation would completely bog down and neither the Hattoris nor Andrew and I would understand what we were talking about. It was at moments like this when Mr. and/or Mrs. Hattori would consult their large English/Japanese dictionary, throw in a few English key words and we would all be in business again.

My fears about being in a very formal atmosphere were very quickly dispelled as the Hattoris were so relaxed and easygoing. One of the first things Mrs. Hattori did was to show us how to use the washing machine which she said we were welcome to use any time that she did not required it. Because the Hattoris with their young son Takashi, who at the time was only 3 years old, lived completely on the ground floor of the house, Andrew and I had the whole upstairs to ourselves, with a large room each. We soon became accustomed to sleeping on our futons, rolled out on the *tatami* mat floor, and it was a joy to wake up each lovely sunny morning to the sound of birds and the nearby breaking sea, slide back the screens in our windows and look out at all the neighbouring houses and picturesque gardens.

Because I am around 6' 2" and Andrew around 5' 9" tall, we appeared like giants to the Hattoris, who, like most Japanese, are quite short. Mrs. Hattori was always worried whether we were getting enough to eat and that we liked the Japanese dishes she prepared for us, but she need not have worried, because her cooking was excellent and she introduced us to many new delicious, previously unknown culinary delights.

The Hattoris family did far more for the two of us than was required by their agreement with Eurocentre, which was just to provide us with accommodation and two meals per day. They took us on all sorts of interesting excursions around Kanazawa City and the surrounding districts, showing us the many aspects of local life and culture. As I came to know them better, especially in my second months after Andrew returned home to the U. S., leaving me on my own, I realized what lovely kind people they were and how much in agreement I was with their view of the world and whole general philosophy. Many of my fellow Eurocentre students had similar experiences and equally high opinions of their host families, too. All of us felt that they all showed great courage in the first place, by even deciding to volunteer to become host families to foreigners from the other sides of the world whose culture and way of life was so different from their own. Whilst at Kanazawa I also gained a second host family during an Eurocentre weekend excursion to Yoshinodani, a beautiful mountain village about 40 km outside the city. There were about 15 of us in the group and each of us was taken into the home of one of the local people who had volunteered to be a host family for that weekend. The Nakanishi family, who looked after me, was again very nice people with a lovely home set amid beautiful mountain scenery who showed me a wonderful time then and again in 1992 when I spent another month at Eurocentre Kanazawa.

Since that time I have kept in touch with my two host families (especially the Hattori family), and we have regularly exchanged letters, cards, presents, family photos, etc. In 1994 I toured the northern parts of Japan, slowly working my way south to Kanazawa where I intended to spend about a week, staying in a hotel, so as not to impose upon the Hattori family at what might have been an inconvenient time for them, using it as a base to visit my two host families, Eurocentre and other local friends I had made through Eurocentre. When I phoned at rather short notice from Niigata, where I was staying at the time, the Hattoris would not hear of this and insisted that I stay with them and even arranged to meet my train on arrival. Again they showed me wonderful hospitality, while I used their home as a base for renewing my friendships with many friends around Kanazawa. Because there was insufficient time to visit Yoshinodani, the Nakanishi family drove into town one night and took me out for a beautiful meal at a lovely restaurant.

In retrospect I would say that my time living with my Japanese host families has been one of the nicest, most interesting parts of my life and I have gained so much from the experience. The staff at Eurocentre Kanazawa did a wonderful job in teaching us Japanese without using English (except maybe very occasionally to make a grammatical point clear.) I learned a great deal and gained so much confidence in using the language, but excellent as the Eurocentre method is, I feel that the organization brings about a far more profound result than the mere gaining of linguistic expertise.

I consider that the real outcome of an Eurocentre course is a move by all the participants, teachers, host families and students toward better international understanding. Not only did I learn so much about Japan, its language and people, but I also met fellow students from many other parts of the world and discovered much about their countries and ways of life too. In view of the tragic sad troubles affecting certain parts of the world at the present time, the more we can get together, as at Kanazawa, and understand one another, the more chance there is of one day attaining peace throughout the world.

SECTIONS: The Land of the Rising CromChris Cote Explores the Many Mysteries of Japan

In 1968 Andy Warhol predicted that in the future, everyone would be famous for 15 minutes. In March of this year, 19-year-old Encinitas ripper Chris Cote (ko-tay) took a trip to Japan and was famous for 10 days. Does this mean Japan is the future, or does it mean that Japan doesn't have a clue? Cote can't answer any of these questions, but he can tell you what not to order at restaurants in Tokyo. Here's his story:

A year ago I had no sponsors, and then it happened all at once. Jeff Moore from Ezekiel Clothing called my house one day and out of the blue he say, "Cote, you're the man. You're going to Japan." After three hours of screaming, I got excited.

A week later I woke up on a Monday and called Ezekiel: "What time should I be there on Friday?" Jeff Moore returned, "What Cote? Be here at 9 this morning. You leave today."

"OK," I calmly replied, then hung up the phone and started screaming again. It was 7:30 AM and I live an hour from the Ezekiel factory. I grabbed my board bag and threw in some semi-clean shirts, one pair of pants, a sweatshirt, some trunks and my passport. Then I wrote a note to my mom. It said:

"Mom, Hey, I'm in Japan. See you soon, ♥ - Chris"

At the factory I met Donavon "Big, Tall and Hairy" Frankenreiter and Vince de la Pena. I felt cool, even when they made me lie down in the back of the truck all they way to LAX.

Two sleeping pills and 10 hours later we landed in Japan. First impression: confusing. As we drove toward Tokyo I couldn't help but think of *Bladerunner*. Tokyo looks exactly like *Bladerunner* town. That night Donavon started going off about the blankets: "Three inches thick. The blankets are three inches thick." I was laughing and couldn't stop, so they made me sleep in the basement.

We were up the next day and went surfing. The waves were about 4-foot. Kinda mushy. Everyone started to smiled at us. On my first wave I poped an air in front of a group of bodyboarders. They started screaming and cheering. I was stoked, and couldn't help but laugh. Donavon would take off and every single person out there would spin around and check him out. Donavon likes to go vertical. He shreds. Vinnie goes fast like a race car.

132

We went to our first shop and right when we got there, three kids asked me for my autograph. They all knew who I was. I was so nervous I spelled my name wrong on the first two autographs. After about 10 shops I was into the autograph deal, and I could sign my name in about one second. In Japan everyone knew who I was. I don't even know who I am.

That night we went to Tokyo to see some clubs. The first place we went to was a mall. There were so many rad girls I got dizzy from the blood loss.

I saw a sumo wrestler. Sumo wrestlers are like kings in Japan. They can get any chick they want.

Then we went to a sketchy S&M club called Mild. There were naked girls painted on the walls, giant blow-up dolls, barbed wire, dildos and stank girls everywhere. I was scared but I got into it. I felt weird, but cool. By about 1 in the morning we left to go home. But Donavon still wanted to party, so we went to Denny's.

In Japan, Denny's rules. The place was filled with chicks. The menu was in Japanese with pictures. I pointed to some pictures. They brought back pancakes, an ice cream sundae, french fries and rice. Never try to eat pancakes with chopsticks. They also were sushi at Denny's.

The next morning we hopped on the Bullet Train bound for Osaka. That thing is fast. In Osaka we walked into this huge, five-story surf shop complete with DJ, bar, record store, halfpipe and beautiful models in bathing suits. I was feeling lucky so I started talking to the swimsuit models. I couldn't understand anything they said, but apparently they were stoked on my whole blond-hair, blue-eyed deal. At about 12, I got separated from the group with this rad girl, Akiko. We went to this club, just me and her, and this place was going off. We were dancing for hours even though I'm so bad at dancing it's not even funny. Actually I'm so bad it *is* funny. If I ever write an article for *Playboy* I'll tell you about Japanese girls and how perfect they are.

The next morning we woke up and went to Shizuoka. By this time Vinnie was going crazy with homesickness. We grinded, went to a surf shop and watched *Good Times*. I wasn't in it, but watching it got me so amped to go surfing. A whole group of us went to the beach. The waves were about 5 inches. Donavon and Vinnie made me surf. It was sort of fun.

The next day there was a pretty big contest called the Breaker Out, Ezekiel Users Cup. The waves were 7 inches. I won. I think I was pushed. In the final I did an air and people screamed. I might have claimed it, but I hope not.

The next day we went back to Tokyo. That night we ate at some real fancy restaurant. I didn't know what to get again so I pointed to something. It turned out to be raw baby squid and fried octopus. The octopus wasn't so bad but the squid's brain exploded in my mouth when I bit into it. I almost puked but I pretended it was cool.

After dinner we did karaoke. Karaoke is my new favorite thing. Vinnie started it off with *Hotel California.* I sang *Roxanne,* then *House of Rising Sun.* For the finale Donavon and I did duet of *Sunshine of Your Love.* Donavon was pretty drunk and when we got home he called his girlfriend at 3 a.m. and talked babytalk to her for three hours. I've never seen a grown-up tough guy sound like such a sissy. His girlfriend was laughing at him the whole time. Even her mom was laughing.

The time finally came to leave Japan and I wasn't happy about it. I was pouting. Many sleeping pills and lost hours later, I was home. I walked into my house and my mom screamed, "Chris! Where have you been?"

I said, "Didn't you get my note?"

Re-printed with a permission from the author. Chris Cote is a surfer living in Encinitas, California. This article appeared in *SURFER* magazine.

Ethnic Japanese find tightly closed society
Some Can't Go 'Home'
Ethnic Japanese find shut society

By Patrick Harrington
Mercury News Tokyo Bureau

SAITAMA, Japan, Wednesday, July 30, 1997 – Stoically enduring the shoves of passengers forcing their way onto a crowded commuter train, Luis Adaniya is just another Japanese face in the vast salaryman sea of Tokyo's suburbs.

But when he speaks, passengers cast lingering, sidelong stares, and a young woman with tinted hair and trendy platform shoes quietly abandons her adjacent seat to stand in the next car.

"When you have a Japanese face and you don't speak Japanese, people think something's wrong with your head," said Adaniya, the roller-coaster intonations of his native Spanish crashing over the quiet background of monotone Japanese.

Adaniya is one of about 250,000 ethnic Japanese from Peru, Brazil and other Latin countries who came to this insular, homogenous nation to seek high-wage jobs and re-establish ethnic ties.

But while they expected a warm reception because of their Japanese appearance and heritage, many find just the opposite. Though genetically Japanese, co-workers often shun them, labor brokers and employers exploit them, and even shopkeepers treat them poorly when they try to buy groceries.

"What shocked me the most," said Adaniya, 41, "is that when I came to the country of my ancestors, they not only treated me as an inferior, but they treated me as an inferior to other foreigners.

"In Peru, I was considered Japanese. People of Japanese origin were treated more like family. To be treated here like something strange is somewhat shocking."

The experience of Adaniya and thousands of other ethnic Japanese demonstrates that despite this country's efforts to internationalize as it has become more prosperous, it remains one of the world's most homogenous societies where outsiders are often shut out. But Adaniya's troubled experience also helps illustrate the unique way Japanese see themselves as different from others.

"If you are a white person, you don't need to speak Japanese. Everyone will help you. But if you have a Japanese face, everyone expects a lot more, and no one wants to help you,' said Adaniya, who emigrated from Lima, Peru, in 1992.

Japanese first came to Peru and Latin America as farm laborers in the early 19th century; a bid wave of immigration came after World War I. From farming, later generations moved into business.

Japanese-Americans constitute the largest group of overseas Japanese, followed by those from Brazil and Peru. Yet foreigners represent a mere 2 percent of the Japan's population – a number that includes people who would not be considered foreigners in the United States, like ethnic Koreans and Chinese who were born here but are essentially deprived of citizenship. As Japan ages and runs out of workers for its factories, and as rising wages force many factories to move overseas, the nation faces more pressure to bring in labor from abroad.

That's how workers like Adaniya got here.

He and thousands of other ethnic Japanese were invited here to help work in the factories and do the dirty, dangerous work that increasingly prosperous Japanese shun. In 1990, the Japanese government changed its immigration law to specifically attract foreign workers with Japanese blood.

The Japanese government would not provide a breakdown on the numbers of male and female Latin-Japanese immigrants. But the International Press, a Spanish- and Portuguese-language weekly newspaper covering the Latin-Japanese community, estimates the breakdown at 70 percent men and 30 percent women. The paper says the number of women is increasing, mostly for jobs in the food-processing and clothing industries.

The government sought to attract ethnic Japanese workers because their familiarity with Japanese culture "would make it easier for them to adjust to Japanese society," according to labor specialist Haruo Shimada, a Keio University professor and author of "Japan's Guest Workers."

But, as Adaniya points out, being an ethnic Japanese who doesn't understand Japan puts him in ethnic limbo.

"There is a double standard," he said. "If a Japanese workers is using a machine that breaks down, the machine just broke down. But if a foreign worker is using it, it's because they did something wrong."

And while his factory provides lunch to the Japanese workers, the foreign workers must pay for their own.

Jose Llompart, a law professor from Spain at Tokyo's Sophia University, has written two books on Japanese self-identity. He says that life in Japan is easy for whites because of what he calls the "myth" of *Nihonjinron* – a belief that Japanese culture is uniquely different from other cultures. Because many Japanese believe it is extremely difficult, if not impossible, for foreigners to adapt to Japanese culture, no one expects them to. On the other and, ethnic

Japanese are often scorned because they act differently from Japanese born in Japan, he said.

"Those poor people,' he said, "they look Japanese but they really are not."

Luis Mitta, 24, came to Tokyo from Lima two years ago. He moved in with his sister, who warned him that life in Japan was not as easy as the advertisements in a Peruvian-Japanese newspaper suggested. He hoped that he could save enough money to return to Lima and open a small business or a bakery as his uncle had.

"Before I came here, I was really proud of being Japanese," he said, especially the success of ethnic Japanese in Peruvian business and politics, such as Peruvian President Alberto Fujimori. "But when I got here, I realized that what I thought was Japan doesn't exist – at least not for me."

After struggling with three employers to receive the salary that promised him and constantly being asked why he could not speak fluent Japanese, Mitta says he "hates" Japan.

"I was angry at first," he said "but now I just want to save money and go home."

Hiroshi Nomura, a manager of Japan's Industrial Employment Stabilization Center, which counsels Japanese workers, admitted that many companies have mistreated ethnic Japanese workers. Most firms use third-party contractors to hire the workers in South America, he said, which means they can deny responsibility when problems arise. But Nomura said the contractors often exaggerate the pay and conditions they offer prospective workers.

Once the workers arrive in Japan to find cramped housing and lower pay then promised, many want to return home, he said. To prevent them from leaving companies often demand workers' passports on arrival. To help protect the immigrants, the government has set up help centers to answer complaints and to pressure companies to adhere to Japanese laws. But Nomura said the government has had only partial success because nearly half the immigrants choose to work illegally rather than pay for Japan's mandated insurance, which is costly.

While Latin-Japanese face work place discrimination, sometimes the social stigma is more painful. At Salsa Caribe, one of Tokyo's handful Latin bars, groups of Japanese look curiously from tables lining the wall while diplomats from the Dominican Embassy twirl and dip women across the floor.

Alone at the bar, Carlos Fujiwari sips on a Corona beer, then warmly greets a friend in Spanish with hearty handshake.

Fujiwari, 27, said he has lived in Japan for four years and has held three jobs. Though he has studied Japanese since arriving from Lima and can hold a conversation, he said co-workers still treat him with suspicion and ask him why he cannot speak Japanese.

As he watches a white man utter a few pidgin Japanese phrases to a Japanese woman and bring her out onto the dance floor, he shakes his head.

"I envy him," he said "Life for him here must be so easy."

Index

American myth
  Japanese men mistreat women..................52
Anne Neumann
  my relationship with................................55
  reasons for my resentment against............56
  Sweetheart Deals...................................110
Anti-Discrimination Clause........................95
Asian Triangle..78
Carolyn Lattin
  confrontation with..................................60
  Sweetheart Deals...................................110
Chris Cote...18, 104
community chest...................................24, 31
Dana Jourdan...19
  meeting for the first time.........................19
  Sweetheart Deals 110
differences between the U. S. and Japan
  individualism *vs.* collectivism.............23, 38
Employment contract................................122
English language schools in Japan
  GEOS..73
  NOVA..73, 74
gaijin
  compared to *die Aüslander*.........................20
  examples of discrimination against...74, 100
  June 22, 1994..21
hanko..108
Harmony*("wha")*......................................49
Hidden Cost Clause....................................96
Japan
  its brand of racism..................................39
  its perception of disputes........................42
  life in...22
  my cultural *faux pas* in...........................23
  its society...23

positive points of living and working
  in..108
  white supremacy in....................................18
Jean-Christian de La Chevalerie....16, 19, 21,
23, 27, 32, 34, 54, 63, 66, 82, 87, 95, 109
  his analysis of the outcome of the Oscar
  Godoy fiasco...51
Kathy Ho..61
  Ghost of Kathy Ho Past..........................102
  my suspicion on her abrupt resignation....59
Kobe Earthquake of 1995...........................109
Luis Adaniya.......................................18, 135
Masaharu Takahashi, Mr.............................90
  his reaction to my dispute with Oscar
  Godoy...43
  his reaction to my law suit against Oscar
  Godoy...49
  meaning of Japanese "yes"........................49
Monica Lennie
  fax to...120
Noa D'ror...77
NTT telephone bond.....................................22
Olivier Japiot...................................43, 61, 89
Oscar Godoy...37
  advertisement for Macintosh sale.............41
  buying Macintosh computer from.............41
  confirmation of my suspicion on his motive
 47
  dispute with..41
  end of the saga with....................................50
  his connection to Macintosh computer.....40
  meeting...40
  meeting once again after a year.................45
  my perception of the dispute with.............45
  search for his home address.......................47

showdown with..46
  three major wrong assumptions about.......42
Peter Shepard.....................................18, 104
  Fond Memories of Life with a Host Family
....128
Places in Roppongi
  Baccarat...71
  One-Eyed Jack...............................77, 79
    white women working at.....................82
Places in Shibuya
  Garden of Eden..................................76
  Hachiko......................................82, 83
  New York...76
Queen Bees
  Anne Neumann..................................55
  Carolyn Lattin...................................60
Rush Limbaugh.......................................52
Ryo Yamanish.........................69, 74, 105
Shiseido
  history of...15
  its backwardness of computer technology 39
  Omori International Headquarters
    effects of introducing Macintosh
    computers at.......................................44
      guide to...6
        organizational chart..............................92
        President Kennedy Speech at................25
Shiseido Nippacho *Mes Amis* dormitory
  behavior report....................................33
  community chest at...............................31
  first arrival on July 20, 1993....................28
  layout..36
  Trash Day...34
  TV Room..35
  food service at.....................................33
Shiseido Girls...16
Smoke Free Clause..................................97
Takahiko Suwa, Dr...................................40

Tatsuya Ozawa, Dr...............................26, 35
  his reaction to my law suit against Oscar
  Godoy..48
  my letter to..112
Toru Arai, Mr.......................................
  description of..116
  outburst on July 23, 1994.......................86
  wha..89
Tyler Thoreson.......................18, 104, 126
White women in Japan
  Amanda Kidd.......................................68
  Anne Drew...76
  Anne Neumann.....................................54
  Carolyn Lattin......................................60
  Christine Morrison.................................75
  Dana Jourdan.......................................63
  Elaine Corbett......................................73
  four classes of 53
  Holly H. Williams.................................73
  Jasmine Bordeaux.................................77
  Jennifer Harmata..................................69
  Kathy Gunn...71
  Kerry...66
  Megan Dorherty....................................66
  Patricia...82
  Shawna S. Mund...................................71
  Shelly..80
  two Australian women.............................81
  their position in Japanese society..............52
  their racial protocol...............................53
Yoshiyuki Nagai, Mr................................34
Yukihara Kanda, Mr................................28
  description of..117
  his mistreatment of me...........................29
  his reaction to my law suit against Oscar
  Godoy..51
William Jefferson Clinton...........................15

Bibliography

Bacharach, Samuel B. and Lawler, Edward J. *Power and Politics in Organizations.* San Francisco, California: Jossey-Bass, 1980.

Baldwin, David A. "Power and Social Exchange." *The American Political Science Review* 72, 1978: 1229 – 1242.

Cook, Curtis W., Hunsaker, Phillip L. and Coffery, Robert E. *Management and Organizational Behavior,* 2nd Edition, IRWIN/McGraw-Hill, 1997.

Crosby, Faye. "A model of egotistical relative deprivation." *Psychological Review*, 1976, 83: 85 – 113.

Crosby, Faye. "Relative deprivation in organizational settings." *Research in Organizational Behavior,* 1984, 6: 51 – 93.

Dalma, Heyn. "Waiting a man out." *New Women,* December 1998, p. 67.

Folger, Robert. "Rethinking Equity Theory: A Referent Cognitions Model," in *Justice in Social Relations.* Eds. Hans Werner Bierhoff, Ronald L. Cohen, and Jerald Greenberg. New York, New York: Plenum, 1986: 145 – 162.

Fortado, Bruce. "The Accumulation of Grievance Conflict." *Journal of Management Inquiry 1,* December 1992: 288.

Hartley, Robert F. *Management Mistakes and Successes.* New York, New York: John Wiley & Sons, Inc., 1997.

Hui, C. Harry and Triandis, Harry C. "Individualism-collectivism: A study of cross-cultural researchers." *Journal of Cultural Psychology,* 1986, 17: 225 – 248.

Leung, Kwok. "Some determinants of conflict avoidance." *Journal of Cross-Cultural Psychology*, 1988, 19: 125 – 136.

Mayes, Bronston and Allen, Robert W. "Toward a Definition of Organizational Politics." *Academy of Management Review 2.* October 1977: 672 – 677.

Morrison, William F. *The Prenegotiation Planning Book.* New York, New York: John Wiley & Sons, Inc., 1985.

Pfeffer, Jeffrey. *Managing with Power: Politics and Influence in Organizations.* Boston, Massachusetts: Harvard Business School Press, 1992.

Runciman, Walter Garrison. *Relative Deprivation and Social Justice.* Berkeley, California: University of California Press, 1966.

Thompson, Leigh L. *The Mind and Heart of the Negotiator.* Upper Saddle River, New Jersey: Prentice Hall, 1998.